THE SERMON-CONFERENCES OF ST. THOMAS AQUINAS
ON THE APOSTLES' CREED

THE SERMON-CONFERENCES OF ST. THOMAS AQUINAS ON THE APOSTLES' CREED

Translated from the Leonine Edition
and edited and introduced by
NICHOLAS AYO, C.S.C.

Wipf & Stock
PUBLISHERS
Eugene, Oregon

Wipf and Stock Publishers
199 W 8th Ave, Suite 3
Eugene, OR 97401

Sermon-Conferences of St. Thomas Aquinas on the Apostles' Creed
Edited by Ayo, Nicholas R.
Copyright©1988 by Ayo, Nicholas R.
ISBN: 1-59752-027-6
Publication date 1/25/2005
Previously published by University of Notre Dame Press, 1988

Translated from the Leonine Edition and Edited and Introduced by Nicholas Ayo, C.S.C.

This book is dedicated to my sister

ALIDA ANN AYO MACOR

whose own book encouraged me to begin my own

CONTENTS

	Acknowledgments	ix
	Introduction	1
I.	I Believe in One God, and So Forth	17
II.	I Believe in One God	27
III.	The Father Almighty, Maker of Heaven and Earth, of All Things Visible and Invisible	35
IV.	And in Jesus Christ, His Only Son Our Lord	45
V.	Who Is Conceived by the Holy Spirit, Born of the Virgin Mary	55
VI.	Suffered under Pontius Pilate, Was Crucified, Was Dead, and Was Buried	65
VII.	He Descended into Hell	77
VIII.	On the Third Day He Rose from the Dead	87
IX.	He Ascended into Heaven, and Sits at the Right Hand of God the Father Almighty	95
X.	From Where He Will Come to Judge the Living and the Dead	103
XI.	I Believe in the Holy Spirit	113
XII.	The Holy Catholic Church	123
XIII.	Communion of Saints, Forgiveness of Sins	133
XIV.	The Resurrection of the Flesh	143
XV.	Eternal Life. Amen.	151
	Notes to the Latin	161
	Notes to the English Translation	163
	Appendix I: Divisions of the Apostles' Creed	169
	Appendix II: Versions of the Apostles' Creed	187

ACKNOWLEDGMENTS

The author would like to thank the many people who made this work possible. I am grateful to my family, especially my ninety-four-year-old mother, who still encourages her children, as well as to my religious family, the Congregation of Holy Cross. In particular, I would thank the Leonine Commission and Father Louis J. Bataillon, O.P. for their indispensable assistance. The Notre Dame Press and John Ehmann and Ann Rice deserve special mention, along with the generous and unknown reader of my typescript. The Wilbur Foundation and Russell Kirk assisted me with a grant. Walter Nicgorski and Philip Sloan of the Program of Liberal Studies at the University of Notre Dame gave me every assistance. Juliette LaChapelle and Suzanne Lutz helped me with editing the text. Cheryl A. Reed, Nila V. Gerhold, and Nancy A. Kegler in the stenopool gave many hours to preparing the text. I would thank so many people who befriended me: Dave Burrell, C.S.C. and Bill Dohar, C.S.C., Mary Catherine Rowland and Macrina Wiederkehr, O.S.B. To all of them, and to many others unmentioned, I am grateful for the composition of this work.

INTRODUCTION

Lent of 1273

Not much is known about Thomas Aquinas as a preacher, nor do we have many of his authentic sermons. The "Collationes Credo in Deum,"[1] which might be translated *sermon-conferences on the creed*, are classified both by Eschmann[2] and Weisheipl[3] as sermons. Previously they had been classified as theological *opuscula*, largely because they were gathered in the volumes of that designation. What is known of these sermons, rather longish and patterned more on the thirty-minute retreat conference of our own day than on the Sunday homily?

We know that Thomas was ordained to the priesthood in 1250 and that his vocation as sermon-writer and preacher probably began at that time. Eschmann thinks that "St. Thomas preached assiduously, as may be expected from a Friar Preacher and, more especially still, a mediaeval Master of Theology whose statutory obligations included preaching just as attendance at University sermons was obligatory for the students" (pp. 425–26). Weisheipl writes:

> Little can be said at this time about Thomas's preaching career during his first Parisian Regency [1250–59]. One of the serious obligations of masters was to preach sacred doctrine. University sermons were always in Latin, and they were listed in the university calendar. Even bachelors had to preach a specified number of times before they could incept in theology. There were, of course, other types of sermons. Some were preached in the vernacular for the faithful, such as during Lent or other times when a series of vernacular sermons was called for. Very often a vernacular sermon or series was organized first in Latin, with the particular points to be preached and the biblical examples to be used in illustration included. Many of these sermon notes have survived in Latin, but the vernacular texts seem to be lost. (p. 128)

Thomas gave just such a series of sermons in the Lent of 1273,[4] about

1

a year before he died. This Lenten cycle almost surely included his conferences on the Apostles' Creed and the Lord's Prayer, some twenty-six sermons, or twenty-eight if the two sermons on the Hail Mary are here included. They were preached daily by Thomas in the parish church of San Domenico Maggiore, in Naples, probably in the late afternoon. Witnesses at the canonization proceeding for Thomas in 1323 recall that these sermons were well attended and well received by many people, both students and ordinary faithful. Thomas preached in the Neapolitan vernacular dialect that was his mother tongue. His sermon-conferences were recorded by Reginald of Piperno, his long-time secretary and companion, who presumably translated them into Latin, very likely after the death of Thomas.

Several commentators think the Lenten series of 1273 also includes the thirty-one conferences on the Ten Commandments. Accordingly, it is argued that the series began on Septuagesima Sunday, February 2, and continued to Wednesday of Holy Week, April 6.[5] Almost sixty conferences in one Lent, however, would have been a heavy schedule for one preacher. Moreover, the evidence that the conferences on the Ten Commandments were taken down by Peter d'Andria instead of Reginald, has led to speculation that these conferences were probably given in a Lent some short time before, and plausibly in Rome.[6]

The circumstances in Thomas Aquinas's life at the time of this Lenten cycle of sermons were as follows. He was forty-eight years of age, and still vigorous in the pursuit of his writings. Regent of Theology at the University of Naples, he was also appointed Preacher-General by the Dominican Priory of San Domenico in Naples, where many years before he had taken the religious habit. Naples at this time was under Angevin rule and was known as the Kingdom of Naples; it was part of the Roman province of the Dominican Order. In this office, which he held from 1260 until his death in 1274, Thomas was responsible for arranging and overseeing all of the preaching by the Dominican Order of Preachers in that entire geographical area throughout the church year. In 1273, Thomas himself undertook to deliver in the vernacular the Lenten series for that year. In their totality, the Thomistic Lenten conferences comprise an adult catechism with exposition of the Ten Commandments, the Apostles' Creed, the Our Father, and the Hail Mary.

Some months after delivering these sermon-conferences. Thomas ceased all activity of writing and preaching. On December 6, 1273, Thomas told Reginald that he could write no more. This event has been variously interpreted as a mystical experience of surpassing in-

tensity that made superfluous further theological endeavors, or as a physiological and psychological breakdown of some sort that paralyzed his initiatives, or as some combination of the spiritual and the medical. In fact, Thomas did no more, and he died the following spring, March 7, 1274, at Fossanuova, while en route as a *peritus* for the fourteenth ecumenical council to be held in Lyons. These sermon-conferences on the Apostles' Creed, therefore, remain among the very last compositions of Thomas Aquinas. Collins calls them "his last words." Lent of 1273 was indeed his last Eastertide in this world.

SCRIBES AND REDACTORS

We have seen above that Thomas gave the "Collationes Credo in Deum" in the vernacular, using a sermon format, in a parish church of Naples, in the Lent of 1273. It is reasonably assumed that his secretary-companion, Reginald of Piperno, took down Thomas's words as they were spoken and subsequently translated the vernacular into Latin, very likely after the death of Thomas in 1274. Sorgia cites several manuscripts which claim in an addendum that the Latin text was a translation of the vernacular and that the text was not written down by Thomas himself (p. 6). A secretarial recording of an oral presentation was common practice, and such a *reportatio* of Thomas would seem to account for what has come down to us in manuscript. It is, of course, possible that Thomas had made brief sermon-notes for himself, and delivered the sermons in the vernacular, using these notes all the while. In that case, Reginald may have had both some notes and the fuller vernacular transcript that he himself took down.

We know that Reginald was a faithful and devoted secretary, who kept the manuscripts of Aquinas in good order and diligently promoted them. From 1259 until the death of Thomas, Reginald was at his side. He was Thomas's *socius continuous,* or full-time companion, charged to meet the secretarial needs of the theologian, the valet needs of the man, and the sacramental needs of the monk and priest. Reginald was himself a *lector theologiae* and a fellow Dominican priest of the Roman Province. He was assisted at times by Peter d'Andria, to whom the *reportatio* of the sermon-series on the Ten Commandments has been attributed.[7]

Reginald died in 1290, leaving the entire collection of Thomas's works in comprehensive order, well prepared for the compiling of the Canonization Catalog in 1323 by Bartholomew of Capua. In that official canonical listing of Aquinas's *Omnia Opera,* the "Collationes

Credo in Deum" is numbered 66. Weisheipl, to whom I am indebted for this textual information, indicates that there are 141 extant manuscripts (p. 401). The "De Articulis Fidei," an earlier and shorter commentary on the creed, survives in 277 manuscripts. The second part of this work, which treats the sacraments, has been translated into English by Joseph Collins.[8] The first part of the "De Articulis Fidei," however, has not yet been translated into English.

Some theological works Aquinas wrote in his own hand, and they were transcribed into a legible script for scribal copying by Reginald. Such an autograph work is not common. The Parma and the Vivès editions refer to the "Collationes Credo in Deum" as "Expositio Super Symbolum Apostolorum." The text we have would seem to be a *reportatio,* or an account of what Thomas said rather than of what he wrote. When a *reportatio* was subsequently corrected by the speaker, it was then called a *lectura.* Such a corrected version of the secretary's record resembled more closely a written work of the author. Unfortunately, there is no evidence that Thomas read over Reginald's text. However, Reginald could be trusted to give an accurate and faithful recording of the words of Thomas. Unlike Peter d'Andria, who added to the series on the Ten Commandments from Aquinas's *Commentary on Matthew,* Reginald did not add anything for the missing commentary on the first petition of the Pater Noster in Thomas's series devoted to the Lord's Prayer. Eschmann maintains that the sermons are "Latin *Reportata*" (p. 426). Weisheipl claims that "they are not the full sermon texts" (p. 319). Hyacinthe Dondaine, who has edited the Leonine text for the series on the creed, writes in his introduction that "du sermon de Saint Thomas, nous n'atteignons vraiment que l'écho transmis par le reportateur" (of Saint Thomas's sermon we actually hear only the echo transmitted by the reporter).

The presumption is that each commentary on one article of the creed made up one sermon. The series on the creed was thus composed of fifteen sermons, since the manuscripts indicate some fifteen divisions of the text, following for the most part the twelve traditional articles of the Apostles' Creed. Each sermon shows a tight structure of clear divisions of the subject. The usual explanation is that the text is twice redacted. Reginald translated the vernacular into a theologian's Latin, and either he or subsequent manuscript redactors arranged the material in some further way to resemble a scholastic treatise. Weisheipl claims that all of the Lenten sermons "have been edited to look like scholastic treatises" (p. 357). Hyacinthe Dondaine thinks the authentic sermon style was lost "peu à peu dans la tradition manuscrite, puis imprimée" (little by little in the manuscript tra-

dition and then in the printed tradition). Dondaine calls attention to the manuscripts that contain the concluding call to prayer at the end of each article: "Let us pray to the Lord, and so forth." He suggests that these words are "an echo of the reporter's work" and a "trace of its origin." This call to prayer would seem to be the residue of the oral version of the sermon as it was once delivered in church. Any further expansion of the text and the voiced underlining of words remain forever lost to us. Bataillon and others[9] currently doing research to discover and edit a few genuine sermons of Thomas, which are not in this particular Lenten cycle, have not found a notably different style of writing. Of course, redaction of all the Aquinas manuscripts to resemble the scholastic organization of a text might have occurred.

We should recall that these *collationes* were sermon-conferences, which allowed a more organized exposition of doctrine than the usual homily. These are catechetical instructions for adults, and typically they were not simplistic, short, or question-and-answer in format. Quite likely they were given in the evenings, when more time could be devoted to a leisurely sermon-conference. Sorgia thinks they were delivered prior to the Lenten fast-day supper (or collation), which in turn was followed in Lent with Compline (p. 6). Mandonnet thinks that the *collationes* were "ni traités, ni expositions, mais de courtes prédications, des conférences, au sens alors reçu à Paris" (neither treatises, nor expositions, but short preachings, some conferences, in the sense then understood in Paris).[10] Torrell argues that there is no difference between a *sermo* and a *collatio* but the name and the moment; he also argues for Vespers-time as the likely moment for their delivery.[11]

What then can we conclude? These *collationes* are sermon-conferences, or at least Latin summaries and well-developed outlines of these conferences. The text we have consists of a somewhat abbreviated version of a series of vernacular catechetical sermon-conferences, translated into Latin, and further redacted to conform to an outline format. In the pulpit, Thomas probably elaborated in the vernacular upon these insights. We do not have reason to think we have the *ipsissima verba* of Aquinas, but there is little reason to doubt that we have the genuine thought and content of his discourse. These works are not disputed in their claim to Thomistic authenticity. They more or less adequately give us the mind and heart of St. Thomas Aquinas upon the Apostles' Creed. Torrell concludes in his discussion of the Ten Commandments text, which if anything was more glossed by Peter d'Andria than the text on the creed was changed by Reginald: "In places, the arguments are scarcely drawn out, the citations reduced to their

briefest expression, the references approximated, the conclusions abbreviated. Doubtlessly that does not suffice to call into question the global fidelity of the transmitted text, but does compel us to recognize that the secretary has there left his mark."[12]

LATIN EDITIONS

Prior to the inception of the Leonine edition, the works of Thomas Aquinas were edited as branches from the common stem of the Roman edition, the Piana edition of 1570–71. That "Editio Princeps," completed in the pontificate of St. Pius V, was in turn derived from earlier printed editions, sometimes considered incunabula. What manuscripts these editions might have perused we do not know. From these original printed sources, several modern editions have taken their texts. The Parma edition of 1852–73 is based primarily on the Piana, as is the Vivès (Paris) edition of 1871–80. This latter edition also makes use of some manuscripts, but it is not truly a critical edition. Vivès was some improvement on the Parma, and it conveniently gives in the footnotes the variant readings in comparison with the Parma. These printed editions make up what has been called the "vulgate" of Aquinas's writings.[13] Mandonnet edited anew the Parma edition in the *Opuscula Omnia* (Paris: Lethielleux, 1927), and the Casa Marietti issued the *Opuscula Theologica* (Turin and Rome: Marietti, 1954). In the footnotes, the Marietti edition gives the biblical Vulgate discrepancies, and also lists parallel passages in the *Omnia Opera* of Thomas.[14]

In 1880, Pope Leo XIII created the Leonine Commission, charged to edit a critical edition of Thomas Aquinas, evaluating all the extant manuscripts of all his works. At this time, some forty of a planned fifty folio volumes have appeared. Hyacinthe Dondaine, O.P., has finished editing the Leonine text for the "Collationes Credo in Deum." The other writings destined to appear in the same printed volume, however, have not been finished at this time. The Leonine Commission has allowed me to make use of the typescript, which may undergo further revision before final publication. This text simplifies and somewhat shortens the Aquinas commentary on the creed by dropping later Scripture accretions and various explanatory glosses. It is a trim and authentic text, with the clutter of the centuries stripped away. Some Scripture quotations, especially from Luke and Ephesians are restored. The abbreviated prayer at the end of each article is included. A final paragraph that talks of the divisions of the creed is

placed in the text (the Vivès spoke of it in a footnote). Nevertheless, the difference between the Leonine edition and previous editions does not seem sufficient to mark a revision of Aquinas's "Collationes Credo in Deum." We can be thankful, however, for a text less problematical, critically composed from an exhaustive evaluation of the extant manuscripts, thereby more authentic and closer to the spoken words of Thomas as a preacher.

ENGLISH TRANSLATIONS

The first English translation of Aquinas's "Collationes Credo in Deum" was introduced by Laurence Shapcote, O.P., in his *The Three Greatest Prayers* (London: Burns and Oates, 1937). This book included Aquinas's sermons on the Our Father and the Hail Mary. That first translation was quickly followed in the United States by Joseph B. Collins, who brought out *The Catechetical Instructions of St. Thomas Aquinas* (New York: Joseph F. Wagner, 1939) two years later. With the addition of the Ten Commandments, his book included all the Lenten sermons. Moreover, Collins also translated the second part of Aquinas's "De Articulis Fidei," which is a separate and earlier treatise on the creed. This work remains the only English translation of that short explanation of the sacraments by Thomas Aquinas.

In his translation Collins used the Latin edition by Mandonnet (1927), which was a revision of the Parma edition. He also used alternative readings here and there from the Vivès edition. What Latin edition Shapcote used is not so easy to determine. His translation preceded Collins by two years, and it is clear from the many differences in their translations that Shapcote did not use the Mandonnet edition of Aquinas. He does seem to have followed the Parma for the most part, but even then I would have to say that I cannot see consistent use of any one Latin edition of Aquinas. Shapcote may have supplemented his work with manuscript investigations. Besides many textual variants in the commentary itself, there are some additions and subtractions in the Scripture quotations. Several additions might be noted. For example, Mary and John are mentioned as already beneficiaries of the resurrection. A passage from Origen is added. Nevertheless, the differences between Shapcote and Collins are not particularly significant.

Why Collins should have brought out a translation of the "Collationes Credo in Deum" just two years after Shapcote is not clear. Perhaps the Shapcote translation was found wanting; perhaps the Man-

donnet text was thought particularly deserving. Collins does add considerable material in his book which the Shapcote does not include. It is also possible that Collins had begun his work before the Shapcote translation appeared. I would justify my own translation by appealing to the Leonine Latin edition just accomplished by Hyacinthe Dondaine, O.P., and at this time not yet in print. I am also aware that both of the previous translations are currently out of print and that I have benefitted from their example. My own translation adds yet more notes and commentary.[15]

The Aquinas Text

The Aquinas text is divided into fifteen sections in all of the Latin editions, and it would seem the manuscripts concur. It would be reasonable to assume that each section represents one sermon, and the sermon as actually delivered would have been longer than the manuscript text rather than shorter. The Scripture texts in particular are quite abbreviated. These biblical references apparently represent a secretarial shorthand, and in the delivery the text of the sermon must have been amplified.

Aquinas devotes three sermons to what is generally considered the first article of the creed. The "descent into hell" is given separate status. The "resurrection of the body" and "life everlasting" are not combined to make one article. In short, Aquinas begins his series of sermons with a leisurely discussion of belief in God, and he gives full value to the "descent into hell." Thus he follows the traditional twelvefold division of the Apostles' Creed, but with some amplification of sections as befits the particular sermon occasion. He does not follow either the fourteenfold division he sketches in the *Compendium Theologiae* (no. 295), nor an untraditional twelvefold division that he uses in his earlier and shorter commentary "De Articulis Fidei." Aquinas does explain that division in the last paragraph of the Leonine text of the "Collationes," and that explanation is not found in the previous Latin editions. Both of these schemes depart from the traditional arrangement of the creed in favor of a two-part arrangement: half the articles deal with the divinity of God, and the other half with the humanity of Christ.

In the fourteenfold division, the seven articles on the divinity are: (1) one God, (2) Father, (3) Son, (4) Holy Spirit, (5) creator, (6) justification (includes church, communion of saints), and (7) remuneration (includes resurrection of the body and life everlasting). The seven

articles on the humanity of Christ are: (1) conceived, (2) born, (3) suffered, (4) descended, (5) rose, (6) ascended, and (7) will come to judge. In the twelvefold scheme the six articles on the divinity are: (1) one God, (2) trinity (Father, Son, and Holy Spirit), (3) creation, (4) justification (church and communion of saints), (5) resurrection of the body, and (6) life everlasting. The six articles on the humanity of Christ follow the sevenfold division described above, but combine "conceived" and "born."

The general pattern of each sermon resembles the organization of a scholastic treatise. As in the *Summa*, there is a general introduction, followed by objections, then a resolution. Whether or not Aquinas organized his sermons in such a point-by-point fashion, with argumentative divisions of the topic, is not easily answered. Some of his sermons were given to academics, and Aquinas typically wrote in this pattern. Manuscript editors, however, may also have thought they should tighten up a literary sermon form, had they the opportunity.

The pattern in the "Collationes Credo in Deum" follows this arrangement: (1) general introduction and explanation of the text with argument and illustration, (2) errors, objections, objectors and their position, with Aquinas's responses given immediately (unlike the *Summa*), (3) benefits to be gained from a pastoral and spiritual point of view, and (4) some concluding remarks, summary, and the very first words of a prayer of petition.[16] This concluding prayer may have been much longer, possibly following a customary liturgical pattern for prayers of the faithful.

Aquinas was well acquainted as a theologian with the text of the Bible in the Vulgate edition of St. Jerome, which had been the accepted text for centuries in the church. Bibles would be in manuscript form, with resultant discrepancies, and no doubt Thomas used many different manuscript Bibles depending on his circumstances. There is evidence that he used the Parisian text of the Vulgate regularly. He frequently ends his paragraphs with a Scripture quotation to summarize. Often he seems to be quoting from memory, and sometimes from the liturgy. References to the Bible appear inexact in places, partly because we do not know what if any manuscript Thomas had before his eyes and partly because he may even have used pre-Jerome old Roman versions of the Bible when they were cited in a patristic commentary.

It is not likely that Aquinas knew any Greek, much less Hebrew. Nevertheless, he wrote many lengthy volumes of Scripture commentary. Glossing the biblical text with comments from the church fa-

thers and from theological reasoning was a large part of a theologian's expected task. Thomas Aquinas was a *magister in sacra pagina* (chairholder in biblical studies). His commentaries on Job, on John, and on the Gospels in his *Catena Aurea* are particularly well done. At Naples, at the time he was giving the Lenten sermons on the creed, he was lecturing on the Christocentric reading of the Psalms. That search for the spiritual meaning of the text was a customary exegesis of the Middle Ages. Contemporary scholarship searches more for the literal meaning of the text and for the historical context to support it. Aquinas did not have the benefit of such "higher criticism," and the Vulgate was read generally without critical apparatus. At times these quotations appear as one-sentence proof-texts, but not always. There is little sense of the Scriptures as a text redacted and demanding to be read carefully in context. And yet, he knew the texts from long familiarity, and he had a sense of the overall direction of the whole of the Bible. Aquinas approached the Bible both from his systematic theological framework and from his meditation and prayer as a monk and a holy man.

In his commentary on the creed, Aquinas quotes the Bible about three hundred times. The New Testament is quoted about two hundred times. The Gospels account for seventy of the quotations used. John is quoted about half of the time, and the synoptic Gospels together complete the other half. Mark is quoted the least. Paul is quoted more often than the four Gospels combined. The Epistles most cited are: I Corinthians (18 times), Romans (17), Ephesians (15), and Hebrews (12). Quotations from I Corinthians 15 and from Romans 6 number about half a dozen each. In the Old Testament, the wisdom literature is clearly cited the most: Psalms (29), Wisdom (20), Job (12), Proverbs (8) and Ecclesiasticus (7). The prophets are quoted twenty-eight times, with Isaiah given half that number. The Torah is cited only three times, and two of these come from Genesis. Without doubt, the two works most frequently referred to in the Aquinas commentary on the creed are the Psalms (29) and the Gospel of John (32).

References to patristic texts number only eleven. Augustine is mentioned or quoted six times, and Gregory three. There is a reference to Origen and a quotation from Dionysius. The Augustine references have been located for the most part, but the Gregory have not yet been. It would seem the references are to Gregory the Great. Patristic texts were often quoted by memory from the Divine Office, and sometimes modified by popular usage. I have not found any edition of Aquinas, however, that footnotes the particular work cited. Moreover, it does not seem that Aquinas was acquainted with any of the classic commentaries on the creed, such as Rufinus or Augustine.

THE LEONINE TRANSLATION

In the beginning of his "Contra Errores Graecorum," Thomas Aquinas gives his insight into the work of textual translation. I would like to adopt his words there as a suitable introduction to my own approach to the translation of Aquinas's commentary on the creed:

> The responsibility of a good translator includes capturing what pertains to the catholic faith while preserving the proposition. The translator, however, following the idiosyncracy of the language into which he translates, changes the way of speaking. Thus, it is clear that if those things which were literally said in Latin were put forth baldly, always proceeding word for word, the exposition would be unseemly. (My translation)

Medieval Latin stands somewhere between the complexity and discipline of classical Latin and the less-inflected simplicity and vagary of modern languages.[17] It has one foot in both worlds, and the translator sometimes favors one or the other. The vocabulary in Thomas is relatively small and mostly theological in character. The biblical quotations introduce words that might send a reader to a Latin dictionary. All translations from the Vulgate here are my own. I used the Clement VIII edition: *Biblia Sacra* (Paris: Garnier Fratres, 1868). Aquinas is fond of set phrases, such as "constat autem," and a list of equivalent English renditions was compiled by me. However, in differing contexts I found myself translating even the same words in different ways. In short, the translation tries to capture the heart of the meaning and at times also tries to stay very close to the literal Latin text. I cannot give a rule that will assist the reader to determine when the text called for a free translation and when not. I hope the result is readable, and I trust that I remain faithful always to the author's intent.

Square brackets are used to indicate material that I have added as editor rather than translator. Parentheses indicate material found in the Aquinas text, but material that might be set apart for the sake of clarity. I have also introduced a numbering system with decimal subdivisions to make clear the divisions of an argument. Aquinas almost always gives some indication that he is passing over to yet another point in a series of observations. However, divisions within a division become bewildering, and the numbering system seemed to me an advantage for the reader.

Notes have been put at the end of the text, because they do not add information that is critical for a first reading. Commentary upon each article of the creed remains brief so as not to distract from the

primary text. These comments precede each division. They are designed to remove some of the obstacles that a contemporary reader might experience when reading Aquinas and also to highlight some topics of particular note.

In this translation I have tried to avoid sex-exclusive language in a very thorough way. Many judgment calls were made, and I pray the reader's indulgence in a matter where English usage is even now being determined. Sometimes the plural was used to avoid the masculine generic pronoun, and at times the noun was repeated to avoid using any pronoun. More controversial is my adopting of plural pronouns as an acceptable substitute for the generic masculine singular where the antecedent is an indefinite pronoun. For example: "And that is why when anyone is baptized, first they confess faith when it is said to them: 'Do you believe in God?' and so forth." I find this strategy preferable to casting such a sentence always in the plural, or rendering it as "*he or she* should confess faith when it is said to him or her." The National Council of Teachers of English in their *Guidelines for Nonsexist Use of Language in NCTE Publications* claims: "In all but strictly formal usage, plural pronouns have become acceptable substitutes for the masculine singular."

Aquinas often uses the Latin word *homo,* which means human being(s), both male and female. I have translated that noun with "he or she," "human being," "human beings," "men and women," "people," "humanity," "humankind," and "one, anyone, someone." When the Latin has the word *vir,* or a derivative, I have kept the intended masculine reference. When the reader sees the word *man,* they should presume the Latin supports it.

In the biblical quotations, I tended to keep the masculine when the Latin was explicit, even if the original biblical languages might be more inclusive. Thomas quoted from the Latin Vulgate. Moreover, I was reluctant to try to edit Scripture, especially the Old Testament, that is so culture-bound.

With the word *God* I avoid the use of a pronoun, and repeat the noun.

NOTES

1. Thomas here mistakenly thought that the Greek for "symbol" was correctly rendered in Latin as *collatio.* The creed was thus considered a collation of the articles of faith, and Aquinas's *collationes* were a collation, or collection, of comments upon these same articles.

2. I. T. Eschmann, O.P., "A Catalogue of St. Thomas's Works," in Etienne Gilson, *The Christian Philosophy of St. Thomas Aquinas*, trans. L. K. Shook (New York: Random House, 1956), p. 425.

3. James A. Weisheipl, O.P., *Friar Thomas D'Aquino: His Life, Thought, and Works*, rev. ed. (Washington, D.C.: Catholic University Press, 1983), p. 401. For information, biographical or textual, Weisheipl is a scholarly source, to which I am indebted throughout. See also Pierre Mandonnet, "Le Carême de St. Thomas d'Aquin à Naples" in San Tommaso d'Aquino: Miscellanea Storico-artistico (Rome: Società Tipografica A. Manuzio, 1924), pp. 195–212.

4. See *The Catechetical Instructions of St. Thomas Aquinas*, trans. Joseph B. Collins (New York: Joseph F. Wagner, 1939). Collins mistakenly indicates Lent of 1274, p. ix.

5. San Tommaso d'Aquino, *Opusculi Teologico-Spirituali*, intr., trans., notes by P. Raimondo Sorgia, O.P. (Rome: Edioni Paoline, 1976), pp. 5–9. See also Weisheipl above, p. 319; and Mandonnet above, pp. 198–99.

6. See Jean-Pierre Torrell, O.P., "Les *Collationes in Decem Preceptis* de Saint Thomas D'Aquin: Edition Critique avec Introduction et Notes," *Revue des Sciences Philosophiques et Théologiques* 69 (1985):5–40 and 227–63. Torrell gives the evidence for authenticity and date and place of composition. He also discusses the nature of a Latin *reportatio* and the guidelines used in the comparison of extant manuscripts. The non-biblical references are also identified.

7. Ibid.

8. See note 4 above.

9. Louis-Jacques Bataillon, O.P., "Un Sermon de S. Thomas D'Aquin sur la Parabole du Festin," *Revue des Sciences Philosophiques et Théologiques* 58 (1974):451–56 and "Le Sermon Inédit de Saint Thomas Homo quidam Fecit Cenam Magnam" 67 (1983):353–69. See also Mandonnet and Torrell below.

10. Pierre Mandonnet, O.P., "Les *Opuscules* de Saint Thomas d'Aquin," *Revue Thomiste* 32 (1927):121–57, p. 136.

11. Jean-Pierre Torrell, O.P., "La Practique Pastorale d'un Théologien du XIIIe Siècle: Thomas d'Aquin Prédicateur," *Revue Thomiste* 82 (1982):213–45, p. 219.

12. See Torrell, note 6 above, p. 18.

13. "Vulgate" usually refers to the Latin version of the Bible, translated and edited by St. Jerome, which became the common (*vulgus* in Latin) edition in general and official use throughout Western Christendom for a thousand years until the Reformation.

14. The "Collationes Credo in Deum" can be found under the title of "Expositio Super Symbolum Apostolorum" in the Parma (16:97), in the Vivès (27:144), in the Mandonnet (4:349), and in the Marietti (2:191).

15. There are translations in several modern languages. I have used in this introduction Raimondo Sorgia's Italian translation, especially his informative introduction. See note 5 above.

16. Sermon 1 differs in that the section on benefits is given first. Aquinas may have wanted in his initial sermon to capture quickly the hearts as well as the minds of his congregation.

17. For an overview of medieval Latin, I recommend one book: Charles H. Beeson, *A Primer of Medieval Latin* (Chicago: Scott, Foresman, 1925).

THE SERMON-CONFERENCES OF ST. THOMAS AQUINAS

ON THE APOSTLES' CREED

I

This division of the Aquinas commentary concerns the mean-ing of belief. Aquinas affirms the position that knowledge of God which is trust in and love of God surpasses knowledge about God, no matter how erudite. Thus the uneducated old woman knows more about God through faith than the philosopher who reasons about God without trust in God.

To believe in God, and not just to believe that God exists, would seem to be the crucial decision in a person's life. This yes or no to existence and life itself, howsoever this decision is made and under-stood, would seem in principle to determine how all of life's expe-rience will ultimately be appreciated. Aquinas here assumes both the existence of God and revelation from God through Christ.

The Latin text of the "Collationes Credo in Deum" is a Leonine Commission version, edited by Father Hyacinthe Dondaine, O.P., under the general supervision of Father Louis J. Bataillon, O.P. With any final revision It is forthcoming in Volume 44 of the Leonine *Omnia Opera* of Thomas Aquinas. In that volume will be printed the full and elaborate editorial apparatus that the commission has used in the preparation of this critical and definitive Latin text. Because of its length and complexity, that apparatus has not been reproduced in this book.

—I—

Credo in unum Deum etc.

Primum quod est necessarium christiano cuilibet est fides sine qua nullus dicitur uere christianus. Fides autem facit quatuor bona. Primum est quia per fidem anima coniungitur Deo: nam per fidem christianam anima facit quoddam matrimonium cum Deo, Osee ii: "Sponsabo te michi in fide". Et inde est quod quando homo baptizatur, primo confitetur fidem cum dicitur ei: 'Credis in Deum' etc.?, quia baptismus est primum sacramentorum fidei. Et ideo Dominus dicit, Marc. ult.: "Qui crediderit et baptizatus fuerit, saluus erit". Baptisma enim sine fide non prodest. Et ideo sciendum est nullum bonum opus acceptum Deo esse sine fide, Hebr. xi: "Sine fide impossibile est placere Deo"; et ideo dicit Augustinus: "Vbi deest agnitio ueritatis, falsa est uirtus etiam in optimis moribus".

Secundo, quia per fidem inchoatur in nobis uita eterna, que nichil aliud est nisi cognoscere Deum, ut Dominus dicit in Io. Et hec cognitio Dei incipit hic in nobis per fidem, sed perficitur in uita futura in qua cognoscemus eum sicuti est; et ideo dicitur, Hebr. xi: "Fides est substantia rerum sperandarum" etc. Nullus ergo potest peruenire ad beatitudinem, que est uera cognitio Dei, nisi hic primo modo cognoscat per fidem; et ideo Io. xx: "Beati qui non uiderunt" etc.

Tertio, quia fides dirigit uitam presentem; nam homo ad hoc quod bene uiuat, oportet quod sciat necessaria ad bene uiuendum. Et si de-

— I —

I believe in one God, and so forth.

The first thing necessary for any Christian is faith, without which no one can truly be said to be a Christian. Faith, moreover, yields four benefits. (1) Through faith the soul is wedded to God, for through Christian faith the soul achieves a kind of marriage with God: "I will espouse you to me in faith; [and you will know that I am the Lord]" (Hos. 2:[20]).[1] And that is why when anyone is baptized, first they confess faith when it is said to them:[2] "Do you believe in God," and so forth? This is because baptism is the first of the sacraments of faith. Therefore the Lord says: Whoever will believe and be baptized shall be saved" (Mark 16:[16]). But, baptism without faith does not prosper. And therefore it must be known that no good work is accepted by God without faith: "Without faith it is impossible to please God, [and to draw near to God one must believe that God exists and rewards those who seek God]" (Heb. 11:[6]). And Augustine says: "Where acknowledgment of the truth is lacking, there is counterfeit virtue even in the best behavior."[3]

(2) Through faith eternal life is begun in us, which is nothing else than to know God, as the Lord says in John:[4] And this knowledge of God starts in us here through faith, but it is perfected in the future life in which we shall know him as he is. And therefore it is said: "Faith is the substance of the things to be hoped for [and an appeal to things not seen]" and so forth (Heb. 11:[1]). Therefore no one can arrive at the happiness which is true knowledge of God, unless one first comes to know God through faith, as John says: "[Because you have seen me, Thomas, you have believed.] Blessed are those who do not see [and have believed]" and so forth (20:[29]).

(3) Faith guides the present life. In order that anyone live well, it is required that they know whatever is necessary for living well.

19

beret omnia per studium addiscere, uel non posset peruenire, uel post
longum tempus. Fides autem docet omnia necessaria ad bene uiuendum. Ipsa enim docet quod est unus Deus qui est remunerator bonorum et punitor malorum, quod est alia uita et huiusmodi: quibus
scitis allicimur ad bona, uitamus mala, Abac. ii: "Iustus autem meus
ex fide uiuit". Hoc etiam patet quia nullus philosophorum ante aduentum Christi, cum toto conatu suo potuit tantum scire de Deo et de
necessariis ad uitam, quantum post aduentum Christi scit una uetula
per fidem; ideo dicitur: "Repleta est terra scientia Dei".

   Quarto, quia fides est qua uincimus temptationes, Hebr. xi: "Sancti per fidem uicerunt regna". Et hoc patet quia omnis temptatio uel
est a dyabolo, uel a mundo, uel a carne. Dyabolus quidem temptat
ut non obedias Deo nec subiciaris ei; hoc remouetur per fidem, nam
per fidem cognoscimus quod Deus est dominus omnium, et ideo sit
sibi obediendum, Petri v: "Aduersarius uester dyabolus" etc. Mundus
autem temptat uel alliciendo prosperis, uel terrendo aduersis. Sed hec
uincimus per fidem que facit nos credere aliam uitam meliorem ista;
et ideo prospera huius mundi despicimus et non formidamus advuer-
sa, quia docet nos credere alia maiora mala, scilicet inferni, Io. "Hec
est uictoria que uincit mundum" etc. Caro etiam temptat inducendo
ad temptationes presentis uite momentaneas; sed fides ostendit nobis
quod per has, si indebite adhereamus eis, perdimus eternas delectationes. Eph. "In omnibus sumentes scutum fidei" etc.

   Sic ergo patet quod multum est utile habere fidem.

   Sed dicet aliquis quod stultum est credere quod non uidetur, nec
sunt credenda. Dico quod hoc dubium primo tollit imperfectio intellectus nostri; nam si homo posset perfecte cognoscere omnia uisibilia
et inuisibilia, stultum esset credere que non uidemus. Sed cognitio
nostra adeo debilis est quod nullus philosophus potuit perfecte inues-
tigare naturam unius musce; unde legitur quod unus philosophus fuit
triginta annis in solitudine ut cognosceret naturam apis. Si ergo intellectus hominis est ita debilis, nonne stultum est nolle credere de

And if all this must be learned through study, either one cannot complete it, or only after a long time. Faith, however, teaches all those things necessary for living well. Faith itself teaches that there is one God, who rewards good and punishes evil, and that there is another life, and so forth, with which knowledge we seek good and shun evil. "But my just one lives from faith" (Hab. 2:[4]).[5] This much, however, is clear. None of the philosophers before the advent of Christ with all of their striving were able to know so much of God and of those things required for [eternal] life as an old woman knows through faith after the coming of Christ. Therefore it is said: "The earth is full of the knowledge of God [as the encompassing waters of the sea]" [Is. 11:9].

(4) Through faith we conquer temptations: "The saints ruled kingdoms through faith, [established justice, obtained promises, and stopped the mouths of lions]" (Heb. 11:[33]). It is evident that all temptation is either from the devil, the world, or the flesh. Indeed the devil tempts one not to obey God, nor to be subject to God. This temptation is taken away through faith, for through faith we know that God is lord of all, and therefore should be obeyed: "[Be sober and vigilant, because] your adversary the devil [prowls around as a lion seeking someone to devour. Strong in faith, resist him]" and so forth (1 Pet. 5:[8]). The world is tempting, either by enticing us with prosperity or frightening us with adversity. But we conquer this temptation through faith that enables us to believe that there is a better life than this one. Therefore we despise the prosperity of this world and we are not frightened by adversity, because faith teaches us to believe in other greater evils, namely hell: "This is the victory that conquers the world, [our faith]" and so forth (John [1 John 5:4]). The flesh entices by drawing us to the momentary temptations of this present life, but faith shows us that if we unduly cling to these temptations, we shall lose eternal delights: "In all circumstances taking up the shield of faith [with which you will be able to extinguish all the flaming arrows of the iniquitous one]" and so forth (Eph. [6:16]). Therefore how evident that it is very useful to have faith.

But someone might say that it is foolish to believe what is not seen nor ought to be believed. (1) I say that the imperfection of our intellect takes this doubt away, for if we were able to know perfectly all things visible and invisible, it would be foolish to believe what we do not see. But, our knowledge is weak to such a point that no philosopher would be able to investigate perfectly the nature of a single fly. Thus one reads that one philosopher spent thirty years in solitude that he might know the nature of a bee. Therefore, if the human intellect is so weak, is it not foolish to be willing to believe about God

Deo nisi illa tantum que homo potest cognoscere per se? Et ideo contra hos dicitur, Iob: "Ecce Deus magnus uincens scientiam nostram".

Secundo potest etiam responderi quod, dato quod aliquis magister diceret aliquid de scientia sua, et aliquis rusticus diceret illud non esse ita sicut magister diceret, eo quod non intelligeret, multum reputaretur stultum ille rusticus. Constat autem quod intellectus angeli magis excedit intellectum optimi philosophi, quam intellectus philosophi intellectum rustici. Et ideo stultus esset philosophus si nollet credere ea que angeli dicunt, et multo magis si non crederet ea que dicit Deus. Contra hos dicitur Eccli. "Plurima supra sensum hominis" etc.

Tertia responsio est quia, si homo nollet credere nisi ea que cognosceret certe, non posset uiuere in hoc mundo. Quomodo ergo posset aliquis uiuere nisi crederet se alicui? Quomodo etiam crederet quod talis esset pater suus? Et ideo necessarium est quod homo credat alicui de hiis que non potest perfecte scire per se; et nulli est credendum nisi Deo. Et ideo illi qui non credunt dictis fidei non sunt sapientes sed stulti, sicut dicit Apostolus: "Superbus est et nichil sciens" etc. Et propter hoc dicebat Apostolus: "Scio cui credidi" etc.; Eccli.: "Qui timetis Deum, credite illi".

Quarto potest responderi quod Deus probat tibi quod hec que docet fides sunt uera. Si enim rex mitteret litteras cum sigillo suo, nullus esset ausus dicere quod ille littere non processerunt de uoluntate regis. Constat autem quod omnia que sancti docuerunt et tradiderunt nobis de fide Christi, signata sunt sigillo Dei, quod quidem sigillum est illa opera que nulla creatura facere potest nisi Deus; et hec sunt miracula quibus Christus confirmauit dicta apostolorum et sanctorum.

Si tu dicas quod miracula nullus uidit fieri, respondeo ad hoc. Constat quod totus mundus coluit ydola, sicut ipse ystorie paganorum ostendunt; sed modo omnes conuersi sunt ad Christum et sapientes et diuites et potentes et multi, ad predicationem simplicium, pauperum et paucorum, predicantium paupertatem et fugam delectationum. Aut ergo hoc factum est miraculose, aut non. Si miraculose,

only those things that human beings are able to know by themselves? And in counterargument it is said: "Behold God is great, overcoming our knowledge" (Job [36:26]).

(2) One might also respond thus. Let us suppose a teacher who might say something about his or her own science, and a bumpkin who might deny it to be as the teacher says. By the very fact the bumpkin would not understand, he or she would be considered quite foolish. Thus it is that the intellect of an angel surpasses the intellect of the best philosopher more than the intellect of the philosopher surpasses the bumpkin's. And therefore philosophers would be foolish if they were unwilling to believe what angels say, and much more so if they would not believe what God says. In opposition Ecclesiasticus says: "Many things above the sense of human beings [are manifest to you]" and so forth [3:25].

(3) There is a third response. If everyone were willing to believe only those things that they might know with certitude, they would not be able to live in this world. How would anyone be able to live unless they put belief in someone? How would they even believe who their own father might be? And therefore it is necessary that human beings believe someone about those things which they cannot know perfectly by themselves. And no one has to be believed but God. And therefore those who do not believe in the pronouncements of faith are not wise but foolish, as the Apostle says: "Proud such a one and knowing nothing, [wearisome with questions and belligerent with words]" and so forth [1 Tim. 6:4]. And because of this the Apostle would say: "I know in whom I have believed, [and I am sure such a one is able to keep my trust unto that day]" and so forth [2 Tim. 1:12]. "Those who fear God, believe in God" (Eccl. [2:8]).

(4) Finally, one could respond that God proves to you that what faith teaches is true. If a king were to send letters with his own seal, no one would dare to say that this letter did not proceed from the will of the king. Thus it is that everything that the saints taught and handed down to us about the faith of Christ is marked with the seal of God. That seal is indeed those deeds which no creature would be able to do, but only God. They are the miracles whereby Christ confirmed the sayings of the apostles and the saints.

If you say that no one sees a miracle happen, I would reply thus. It is a fact that all the world cultivated idols, as the very history of the pagans shows. But how were all of them converted to Christ, both the wise and the rich, both the powerful and the multitude, by the preaching of simple men who were poor and few in number, preaching poverty and flight from delights? Either this fact is miraculous

habeo propositum. Si non miraculose, dico quod non potuit esse maius miraculum quam quod mundus sine miraculis conuertetur. Non ergo queras aliud

Sic ergo nullus debet dubitare de fide, sed certius debet credere ea que fidei sunt quam ea que uidet, quia uisus hominis potest decipi, sed scientia Dei numquam fallitur.

or not. If it is miraculous, I have made my point. If it is not miraculous, I say that there cannot be a greater miracle than the world should be converted without miracles. No need to search any further.

So therefore no one ought to doubt about faith, but ought to believe those things of faith more surely than those which one sees, because human sight can be deceived, but the knowledge of God is never mistaken.

II

This division of the Aquinas commentary concerns the meaning of God as governor and provider for the natural order and the human order. Christianity has always charted a course midway between a pantheism that denigrates the genuine activity of creation in itself and a deism that evacuates the involvement of God in all events, both in nature and in human freedom. Aquinas insists upon the sovereignty of God, who is the mystery of the infinite One and the created many. The creation, which is not God, remains nonetheless within the providence of God and within the sovereign activity of God's will. God, who made human freedom, moves it from within, without in any way damaging the integrity of the human being in its genuine freedom. In prayers of petition, the Christian community asks not only for those things beyond its capacity to accomplish, but also for its daily bread which requires no extraordinary intervention from God. Aquinas in his commentary insists upon the providence of God in all events, no matter what the secondary causes may prove to be.

Credo in unum Deum.

Inter ea que debent credere christiani, hoc est primum quod credere debemus scilicet quod Deus sit unus. Considerandum est autem quid est dictu hoc nomen Deus, quod quidem nomen nichil est aliud dictu quam gubernator et prouisor rerum omnium. Ille ergo credit Deum esse, qui credit res omnes huius mundi gubernari et prouideri ab aliquo.

Qui autem quod omnia a casu proueniant credit, hic non credit Deum esse. Nullus autem inuenitur adeo stultus qui non crederet quod res naturales gubernentur et prouideantur et disponantur a Deo, cum in quodam ordine et certis temporibus procedant. Videmus enim solem, lunam, stellas et res omnes naturales determinatum cursum habere, quod non contingeret si a casu essent; unde si aliquis esset qui non crederet Deum esse, stultus esset secundum illud Ps. "Dixit insipiens in corde suo: Non est Deus" etc.

Sunt autem aliqui qui licet credant Deum gubernare et disponere res naturales, non tamen credunt uerum esse hominum, illi scilicet qui credunt quod actus humani non disponantur a Deo. Cuius ratio est quia uident bonos in mundo isto affligi et malos prosperari, quod uidetur tollere prouidentiam diuinam circa homines; unde in persona istorum dicitur Iob "Circa cardines celi ambulat, nec nostra considerat" etc.

Hoc est ualde stultum. Nam istis accidit sicut si aliquis nesciens medicinam et uideret medicum propinantem uni infirmo aquam, alteri uinum, secundum scilicet quod ars medicine docet: credit quod hoc fiat a casu, cum nesciat artem medicine qua ex certa causa hoc facit, scilicet quod isti dat uinum, illi uero aquam. Sic est de Deo. Deus enim ex certa sua prouidentia et dispositione scit ea que hominibus sunt necessaria; et ideo aliquos etiam bonos affligit, aliquos

I believe in one God.

Among all the things that Christians ought to believe, the first thing we ought to believe is that there is one God. Let us consider, however, what the name "God" means, that indeed the name means nothing else than governor and provider of all things. Whoever, therefore, believes someone governs and provides for all things of this world believes God to be.

Whoever believes, however, that everything comes forth from chance, does not believe God to be. Nobody, however, is found so foolish as not to believe that natural matters are governed, provided for, and arranged by God, since they proceed in a certain order and within set timeframes. We see that the sun, moon, and stars, as well as all natural matters, have a determined pattern, which would not happen if they were issuing from chance. Thus if there were anyone who would not believe God to be, such a one would be foolish according to the Psalm: "The stupid man said in his heart: there is no God" and so forth [13:1].

There are those, however, who although they may believe that God governs and arranges natural matters, nevertheless do not believe it is true of human affairs. They believe that human acts are not arranged by God. The reason is that they see good people are afflicted in this world and evil ones prosper, which seems to remove divine providence with regard to human beings. Job speaks for them when he says: "[The clouds are his hiding place]. Around the poles of heaven he strolls, and does not consider our affairs" and so forth [22:14].

This is extremely foolish. Consider this parallel. Suppose someone ignorant of medicine would see a doctor offering water to one sick person, to another wine, according to what the art of medicine teaches. They believe that all this happens by chance, since they do not know the art of medicine, which does this for a particular reason, giving wine to one person but water to another. Thus it is with God. God knows from God's own sure providence and arrangement those things which are necessary to human beings. Therefore God

29

etiam malos in prosperitate dimittit. Vnde qui credit hoc prouenire a casu reputatur insipiens, quia non contingit ei hoc nisi quia nescit artem et causas dispositionis diuine, Iob: Ignoras "quod multiplex sit lex eius" etc.

Et ideo firmiter credendum est quod Deus disponat et gubernet non solum res naturales, sed etiam actus humanos, Ps. "Dixerunt: Non uidebit Dominus" etc., "qui docet hominem scientiam" etc. Omnia ergo uidet, et cogitationes et occulta uoluntatis hominis; unde et hominibus specialiter imponitur necessitas bene faciendi, quia omnia que faciunt et cogitant conspectui diuino manifesta sunt.

Est autem credendum quod hic Deus qui omnia disponit et gubernat, sit unus Deus tantum. Cuius ratio est quia dispositio rerum humanarum illa est bene disposita, in quibus inuenitur multitudo disponi et gubernari per unum, nam multitudo presidentium inducit sepe in subditis dissentionem; unde cum regimen diuinum premineat regimini humano, manifestum est quod regimen mundi non est per multos deos sed per unum Deum.

Sunt autem quatuor ex quibus homines inducti sunt ad ponendum plures deos. Primum est imbecillitas intellectus humani: nam homines imbecillis intellectus, non ualentes corporalia transcendere, non crediderunt aliquid esse ultra naturam sensibilem corporum; et ideo inter corpora illa posuerunt preminere et disponere mundum que pulcriora et digniora inter ea uidebantur, et eis attribuebant et impendebant cultum diuinum: et hec sunt corpora celestia, scilicet sol et luna et stelle. Et istis accidit sicut alicui eunti ad curiam regis, uolens uidere regem: credit enim quoscumque uidet bene indutos uel in officio constitutos regem esse. De hiis dicitur Sap. "Solem aut lunam aut gyrum" etc., "maior est" etc.; Ysa. "Leuate in excelsum oculos uestros" etc.

Secundo prouenit ex adulatione hominum. Nam aliqui uolentes adulari dominis et regibus, eis honorem Deo debitum, obediendo eis et subiciendo se eis, impendunt; unde et aliquos post mortem fecerunt deos, aliquos etiam in uita dixerunt deos: Iudith "Vt sciat omnis gens quia non est deus in terra nisi Nabug [odonosor]" etc.

afflicts some good people on one hand, and places in prosperity some bad people on the other hand. Whoever believes that this occurs by chance is considered to be quite foolish, because it is clear that they are ignorant of the art and motives of the divine dispensation: do you not know "[that he might show you the secrets of his wisdom and] how multiform is his law" and so forth (Job [11:6]).

Therefore it must be firmly believed that God arranges and governs not only natural matters, but also human acts: "They said: the Lord will not see [nor will the God of Jacob understand]" and so forth, "who teaches humankind knowledge" and so forth (Ps.[93:7]).[6] Therefore God sees everything, both thoughts and hidden motions of the human will. Thus upon human beings especially is imposed the necessity of acting well, because everything they do and think is manifest to the divine regard.

Furthermore we must believe this God who arranges and governs all things to be only one God. The reason is that in any good ordering of human affairs we find many things are arranged and governed by one person, because too many chiefs often lead to dissension in their subjects. Thus, since the divine regime surpasses the human, it remains clear that the ruling of the world is not through many gods but through one God.

There are four reasons that induce people to posit many gods. (1) The weakness of the human intellect. Persons of weak intellect are not vigorous enough to transcend bodily matters; they would not believe anything beyond the sensible nature of bodies. Therefore they claim preeminence in the arrangement of the world for those beings that seem to be more beautiful and more worthy among bodily things. Upon them they bestow and urge divine worship. These heavenly bodies are the sun and moon and stars. Consider this parallel. Someone goes to the court of the king, wishing to see the king. They believe the king to be whosoever they notice well dressed or holding some office. Wisdom says of this: "Sun or moon or ring of stars" and so forth, "[the one who made them] is greater" and so forth [13:2–4].[7] And "Lift up your eyes on high [and see the earth below. The heavens will vanish like smoke and the earth will be cast aside like a garment . . . but my salvation will be forever and my justice will not fall short]" and so forth (Is. [51:6]).

(2) Human adulation. Some people wishing to flatter lords and kings offer to them the honor due to God, obeying them and subjecting themselves to them. Thus they have made some people gods after their death, and others even in this life: "That all people may know that there is no God on earth but Nabug[odonosor]" and so forth (Jud. [5:29]).

Tertio prouenit ex carnali affectu ad filios et consanguineos. Aliqui enim propter nimium amorem quem habebant ad suos filios, faciebant statuas eorum post mortem; et sic ex hoc processum est quod illis statuis impenderent cultum diuinum. De hoc dicitur Sap. xiii: Omnes "regibus aut affectibus desseruientes incommunicabile nomen" etc.

Quarto ex malitia dyaboli. Ipse enim a principio uoluit in aliquo equiparari Deo, unde et dixit "Ponam sedem meam" etc.; et hanc uoluntatem nondum deposuit. Et ideo totus conatus eius in hoc extat ut faciat se adorari ab hominibus et offerri sibi sacrificia; non quod delectetur in uno cato uel cane qui ei offertur, sed delectatur in hoc quod ei impenditur reverentia sicut Deo. Inde est etiam quod intrantes ydola dabant responsa, ut scilicet uenerarentur ut dii, Ps. "Omnes dii gentium demonia"; Apostolus: Nunc et gens que immolat, demonibus.

Licet autem hec sint multum horribilia, sunt tamen multi qui frequenter in istis quatuor causis incidunt; et licet non corde, factis uero ostendunt plures deos se credere. Nam illi qui credunt quod corpora celestia possint imprimere in uoluntatem hominis, et qui in factis suis accipiunt certa tempora, hii ponunt ipsa corpora esse deos: Ier. "A signis celi nolite metuere" etc. Item omnes illi qui obediunt regibus plus quam Deo, uel in hiis in quibus non debent, constituunt illos deos suos: Act. "Obedire oportet magis Deo quam hominibus". Item omnes illi qui diligunt filios aut consanguineos plus quam Deum, ostendunt factis suis plures esse deos; uel etiam illi qui diligunt se plus quam Deum: de hiis dicit Apostolus "Quorum deus uenter est" etc. Item omnes illi qui insistunt ueneficiis et incantationibus, credunt quod demones sint dii; et ratio est quia petunt a demonibus illud quod solus Deus donare potest, et reuelationem alicuius rei occulte et ueritatem futurorum.

Est ergo primo credendum quod est unus Deus tantum.

Rogemus ergo Dominum etc.

(3) Inordinate affection for family and relatives. There are some people who on account of the excessive love they have for their family make statues of them after their death. And from this it follows that divine worship is offered to these statues. Of this Wisdom says: Everyone "serving either kings or their own desires [imposed] the ineffable name [upon stone and wood]" and so forth (13 [14:21]).

(4) The malice of the devil. He wished from the beginning to be equal to God. Thus it is said: "[I will rise up to heaven; above the stars of God] I will put my seat" and so forth [Is. 14:13].[8] And the devil has not yet put aside this desire. And so all his effort amounts to this that he may make himself adored by humankind and have sacrifices offered to himself. Not that he relishes any dog or cat that is offered to him, but rather he is delighted that to him is given reverence as it is given to God. Thus it is that the devils who entered into idols attested that they would be venerated as Gods: "All the gods of the gentiles are demons" (Ps. [115:5]).[9] And the Apostle says: "But the people who offer sacrifice do so to demons [and not to God]" [1 Cor. 10:20].

Although such practices are quite dreadful, there are nonetheless many people who frequently exemplify these four motives. Although not intending so in their heart, they do show by their deeds that they believe in many gods. Those who believe that the heavenly bodies are able to impress themselves upon the human will, and those who in their activity accept astrological timing, these people indicate those bodies to be gods: "Do not be afraid of the signs from heaven [which the Gentiles fear]" and so forth (Jer. [10:2]). Similarly, everyone who obeys kings more than God, or obeys in matters which they ought not, sets them up as their gods: "We must obey God rather than human beings" (Acts [5:29]). Similarly, all those who love their family or relatives more than God show by their deeds there are many gods. And those who love themselves more than God do likewise. Of these the Apostle says: "Whose belly is their God" and so forth [Phil. 3:19]. Similarly, all those who insist upon magic and incantations believe the demons to be gods. For they petition from the demons what God alone can give, both the revelation of any hidden matter and the truth of future events.

Thus the first thing that must be believed is that there is only one God. Therefore, let us pray to the Lord, and so forth.

III

This division of the Aquinas commentary concerns the meaning of God as the creator of heaven and earth. Aquinas is concerned with the almighty God, who made all things and sustains all things even now. Surprisingly, he makes no mention of God as father-almighty. Much of the rational meaning of the term "father" dwells in the adjective "all-mighty." Aquinas's argument for creation flows from a theory of adequate causality. He argues that where there is smoke there is fire. Thus the beauty and excellence of the world demands a sovereign maker.

The problem of evil in the world might seem to suggest there is more than the one God, who is good, but Aquinas argues that more than one God would eliminate the reality of a sovereign God. The one God made everything; God created time and space from nothing and from the beginning. Evil may be regarded as a puzzle from our viewpoint; it remains a servant from the viewpoint of God's ineffable wisdom.

From this notion of God as creator follows the understanding that God can re-create. Therefore no evil, no death, no tragedy can be final before God. Since God creates and can likewise restore at any time in any way, all of life is a gift, for which the proper response remains to "give thanks always and everywhere." Moreover, it falls to humankind not only to appreciate the world as gift, but to steward the goods of the earth as God would. Human beings, created in the image of God, must act as stewards of God's given and good world.

Patrem omnipotentem factorem celi et terre, uisibilium omnium et inuisibilium.

Sicut dictum est, primum quod debemus credere est quod sit unus Deus; secundum uero est ut credamus quod iste Deus sit formator et creator celi et terre, uisibilium et inuisibilium. Et ut rationes subtiles dimittantur ad presens, quodam rudi exemplo manifestatur propositum, scilicet quod omnia sunt a Deo facta uel creata.

Constat enim quod si aliquis intraret domum quandam, et in introitu ipsius domus sentiret calorem, postmodum uero uadens interius sentiret maiorem calorem, et sic deinceps, crederet ignem esse interius, etiam si ipsum ignem non uideret qui causaret illos calores. Sic ergo contingit consideranti res huius mundi. Nam ipse inuenit res omnes secundum diuersos gradus pulcritudinis et nobilitatis esse dispositas, et quanto magis appropinquat ad Deum, tanto pulcriora et nobiliora sunt; unde celestia nobiliora et pulcriora sunt quam corpora inferiora, et inuisibilia quam uisibilia. Et ideo credendum est quod hec omnia sint ab uno Deo, qui dat singulis rebus suum esse et nobilitatem, Sap. xiii "Vani sunt omnes homines" etc.; "a magnitudine enim creature" etc. Sic ergo pro certo debet nobis constare quod omnia que sunt in mundo isto, creata sunt a Deo.

Circa hoc autem debemus uitare tres errores. Primus est error Manicheorum, qui dicunt quod omnia uisibilia creata sunt a dyabolo, et Deo attribuunt solum creationem inuisibilium. Et causa huius erroris est quia ipsi dicunt Deum esse summum bonum, sicut et uerum est, et omnia que sunt a bono sunt bona. Vnde nescientes discernere quid sit bonum et quid sit malum, crediderunt quod omnia illa que sunt aliqualiter mala, essent mala simpliciter; sicut ignis quia urit

— III —

The Father almighty, maker of heaven and earth, of all things visible and invisible.

As we have said, the first thing that we ought to believe is that there is one God; but the second is that we believe that this God is the molder and creator of heaven and earth, of all things visible and invisible. Let us set aside for the present any subtle reasoning. The proposal that God made or created everything is evident from a simple example.

Thus if someone were to enter a particular house and in the entrance of this house were to feel some heat, yet afterwards going further inside would feel more heat, and so on yet again, they would believe there is fire further on inside, even if they would not see the fire itself which caused the increasing heat. So it stands with anyone considering the being of this world. Such a person discovers that all things are arranged according to various levels of beauty and excellence, and the more one draws near to God, so much the more these things are beautiful and excellent. Thus heavenly things are more excellent and beautiful than bodily things below, and invisible things more than visible. Therefore we must believe that all these things come from one God, who gives to particular things their existence and their excellence: "Hollow are all human beings [who lack knowledge of God and from those things that they see are good cannot understand him who is, nor noting his works acknowledge the artisan]" and so forth (Wis. 13:[1]). "From the greatness [and beauty] of the creature [the creator of these things is intellectually recognized]" and so forth (Wis. 13:[5]). Thus it is with certainty we ought to maintain that all things which are in this world are created by God.

In this matter we ought to avoid three errors. (1) The error of the Manicheans. They say that all visible things are created by the devil, and they attribute to God the creation of invisible things only. The reason for this mistake is that they say God is the highest good, which is true enough, and that everything from good is good. Subsequently, not knowing how to discern what may be good and what may be bad, they believe that all those things which are in any way bad

dicitur ab eis simpliciter malus, et aqua quia necat. Et ideo quia nichil istarum rerum sensibilium est simpliciter bonum, sed ex aliqua parte deficiens, dixerunt quod omnia uisibilia non sunt facta a bono Deo, sed a malo.

Contra hos ponit Augustinus tale exemplum. Si aliquis intraret domum fabri, et inueniret ibi instrumenta in quibus impingeret et lederet se, et ex hoc reputaret illum fabrum malum quia teneret illa instrumenta, stultus esset, cum faber teneat ea ad opus suum. Ita stultum est dicere quod propter hoc creature sint male quia in aliquo sint nocive; nam quod uni est nociuum, alteri est utile.

Hic autem error est contra fidem Ecclesie; et ideo ad hoc remouendum dicitur 'Factorem uisibilium'. Gen. "In principio creauit Deus" etc.; Io. i "Omnia per ipsum facta sunt" etc.

Secundus est error ponentium mundum ab eterno, secundum quem modum loquitur Petrus "Ex quo, inquit, dormierunt patres nostri, omnia sic perseuerant". Et isti ducti sunt ad positionem hanc, quia nescierunt considerare principium mundi. Vnde, secundum quod Rabbi Moyses dicit, istis contingit sicut puero qui, statim cum nascitur, poneretur in insula et numquam uideret mulierem pregnantem, nec puerum nasci; et diceretur isti puero, quando iam esset magnus, qualiter homo concipitur portatur in utero et nascitur: nullo modo crederet, quia uideretur ei impossibile quod homo posset esse in utero matris. Sic isti considerantes statum mundi presentem, non credunt quod inceperit.

Est etiam hoc contra fidem Ecclesie; et ideo ad remouendum hunc errorem dicitur 'Factorem celi et terre'. Si ergo fuerunt facta, constat quod non semper fuerunt; et ideo dicitur in Ps. "Dixit et facta sunt".

Tertius est error ponentium Deum fecisse mundum ex preiacenti materia. Et ad hoc inducti sunt, quia uoluerunt metiri potentiam Dei per potentiam nostram. Et ideo quia homo nichil potest facere nisi ex preiacenti materia, crediderunt quod eodem modo et Deus: unde dixerunt quod in productione rerum habuit materiam preiacentem.

Sed hoc non est uerum. Nam ideo homo nichil potest facere sine

would be bad in all ways. For example, fire which burns and water which drowns are said by them to be bad altogether. Therefore, since nothing of these sensible things is in all ways good, but is deficient in some way, they say that all things visible are not made by a good God, but by a bad one.

In counterargument Augustine[10] gives this example. If anyone were to enter the home of an artisan, and were to find there tools that upon handling injured them, they might from this consider that the artisan was bad for keeping such tools. How foolish they would be, since the artisan keeps them for work. Similarly, it is foolish to argue that creatures are bad because in some instances they are harmful, for what is harmful to one person is useful to another.

This error [of the Manicheans] is opposed to the faith of the church. And therefore it is said to counter it "Maker of all things visible" [see the Nicene Creed]. And "In the beginning God created [everything, heaven and earth]" and so forth (Gen. [1:1]); "Through him everything was made; [and without him nothing was made that was made]" and so forth (John 1:[3]).

(2) The error of those holding the world to be from all eternity. Accordingly, Peter speaks out: "Indeed, our fathers have fallen asleep, and everything remains the same [as it was from the beginning of creation"]. [2 Pet. 3:4]. Consequently, according to what Rabbi Moses[11] says, these people resemble a boy who immediately after birth is placed on an island where he would never see a pregnant woman nor a child being born. This child would be told, when he grew up, just how a human being is conceived, carried in the womb, and born. In no way would he believe it, because it would seem to him impossible that a human being could be in the womb of the mother. Similarly, those considering the present condition of the world do not believe that it could have begun.

This opinion is opposed to the faith of the Church, and therefore to remove this error we read "Maker of heaven and earth" [in the creed]. If therefore all things were made, thus it follows that they were not always. Hence we read: "[Because] he said and they were made; [he gave the order and they were created]" (Ps. [148:5]).

(3) The error of those proposing that God made the world from preexistent material. They come to this conclusion because they wish to measure the power of God in comparison with our power. And thus because human beings are able to make nothing without preexistent material, they believed the same thing of God. Hence they said that in the production of things God had preexistent material.

But this is not true. Although human beings are not able to make

preiacenti materia, quia est factor particularis, et non potest inducere nisi hanc formam in materia determinata ab alio sibi presupposita. Cuius ratio est quia uirtus sua est determinata ad formam tantum, et ideo non potest esse causa nisi huius forme; Deus autem est causa uniuersalis omnium rerum, et non solum creat formam sed etiam materiam, unde de nichilo omnia fecit. Et ideo ad remouendum hunc errorem dicitur 'Creatorem celi et terre'.

In hoc ergo differt creare et facere, quia creare est de nichilo aliquid facere, facere autem ex aliquo aliquid. Si ergo ex nichilo omnia fecit, credendum est quod iterum possit omnia facere si destruerentur; unde potest cecum illuminare, mortuum suscitare et opera miraculosa facere. Sap. xii "Subest tibi cum uolueris posse".

Ex huiusmodi consideratione homo dirigitur ad quinque. Primo ad cognitionem diuine maiestatis. Nam factor preeminet factis; unde quia Deus factor est omnium rerum, constat eum eminentiorem omnibus rebus. Sap. "Quorum si speciem delectati sunt" considerare etc. Et inde est quod quicquid potest uel intelligi uel excogitari, minus est ipso Deo. Iob "Ecce Deus magnus" etc.

Item ex hoc dirigimur ad gratiarum actionem. Quia enim Deus est creator omnium, certum est quod quicquid sumus et quicquid habemus ex Deo est; Apostolus "Quid habes quod non accepisti? Si autem accepisti, quid gloriaris?" etc.; Ps. "Domini est terra" etc. Et ideo debemus ei reddere gratiarum actiones. Ps. "Quid retribuam Domino?" etc., "calicem" etc.

Tertio inducimur ad patientiam in aduersis. Nam licet omnis creatura sit a Deo, et ex hoc sit bona secundum naturam suam, tamen si in aliquo noceant et inferant nobis penam, debemus credere quod illa pena sit a Deo; non tamen culpa, quia nullum malum est a Deo. Et ideo si omnis pena quam homo suffert est a Deo, debet patienter

anything without preexistent material, that is because they are makers of the particular and are not able to draw forth this form without material determined and presupposed from another. The reason is that their own virtuosity is limited to the form alone, and therefore can be the cause only of this form. God, however, is the universal cause of all things, and God creates not only the form but also the matter. Thus God made everything from nothing. Therefore to remove this error we read: "Creator of heaven and earth" [in the creed].

To create differs from to make insofar as to create is to make something from nothing. Therefore, if God made everything from nothing, we must believe God would be able to make everything again were it destroyed. Thus God can illumine the blind, raise up the dead, and do miraculous deeds: "[You are sovereign in power yet you judge with tranquilness, and with great reverence you arrange our affairs;] whatever you may will, you are able to accomplish" (Wis. 12:[18]).

From such consideration one is led to five benefits. (1) Knowledge of the divine majesty. Surely the maker surpasses the made. Since God is the maker of all things, thus it is God surpasses all things. Consider this: "If they are so delighted by the beauty of these things, [that they take them to be gods, let them know how much more beautiful is the lord of them all, for the source of beauty contrived all these things]" (Wis. [13:3]). Whence whatever can be either understood or even thought is less than God himself: "Behold how great God is [exceeding our knowledge; the number of his years is inestimable]" (Job [36:26]).

(2) We are led to give thanks. Since God is the creator of everything, surely whatever we are and whatever we have comes from God. The Apostle says: "What do you have that you have not received? If, however, you have received, why do you glory [as if you had not received]" [1 Cor. 4:7]. And "The earth belongs to God [and its fullness; the globe and those who dwell therein]" (Ps. [23:1]). And therefore we ought to give thanks to God: "What shall I render to the Lord [for everything he has given to me]" and so forth, "the cup [of salvation I will take up, and the name of the Lord I will call upon]" and so forth (Ps. [115:12–13]).

(3) We are led to have patience in adversity. Although every created thing comes from God, and accordingly is good in its own nature, nevertheless if in some way they harm us and bring us pain, we must believe that this suffering is from God. This argument does not apply to sinful guilt, because no evil stems from God. And therefore, if all pain which a human being might suffer comes from God, he ought to endure it patiently, both because it comes from God and

sustinere, et quia est a Deo et quia ordinatur ad bonum; nam pene purgant peccata, humiliant reos, prouocant bonos ad amorem Dei. Iob "Si bona suscepimus de manu Domini" etc.

Quarto inducimur ex hoc ad recte utendum rebus creatis. Nam creaturis debemus uti ad hoc ad quod facte sunt a Deo; sunt autem facte a Deo ad duo: ad gloriam Dei, Prou. "Vniuersa propter semet ipsum", idest propter gloriam suam, "operatus est Deus"; et ad utilitatem hominis, Deut. "Que fecit Dominus Deus tuus" etc. Debemus ergo uti rebus ad gloriam Dei, ut scilicet in hoc placeamus Deo; item ad utilitatem tuam, et hoc quando non facis contra Deum, sicut peccata. Paral. "Tua sunt omnia, et que de manu tua," etc. Quicquid ergo, si scientiam, si diuitias, si pulcritudinem, totum debes referre et uti eo ad gloriam Dei.

Quinto dirigimur ex hoc in cognitionem dignitatis humane. Deus omnia fecit propter hominem, sicut in Ps. dicitur "Omnia subiecisti sub pedibus"; et homo est magis similis Deo inter creaturas post angelos, unde dixit "Faciamus hominem" etc. Hoc enim non dixit de celo nec de stellis, sed de homine; et non quantum ad corpus, sed quantum ad animam que est liberam uoluntatem habens et incorruptibilem, in quo magis assimilatur Deo quam alie creature. Debemus ex hoc considerare homines post angelos digniores esse ceteris creaturis, et nullo modo dignitatem nostram diminuere propter peccata, et propter inordinatum appetitum rerum corporalium que uiliores sunt nobis et ad seruitium nostrum facte. Sed eo modo debemus nos habere quo Deus fecit nos: Deus enim fecit hominem ut preesset omnibus que mouentur in terra, ut subsit Deo. Debemus ergo dominari et preesse rebus, et subesse et obedire et seruire Deo; et ex hoc perueniemus ad fruitionem Dei, ad quam etc.

because the suffering is ordered to the good. Thus, sufferings purge sins, humble the outlaw, and spur the good to the love of God: "If we accept good things from the hand of God, [why would we not accept the bad]" and so forth (Job [2:10]).

(4) We are drawn to the right use of created goods. We ought to use creatures for the purposes they were made by God. They were made by God for two reasons, however. (4.1) For the glory of God: "[The Lord has worked] all things for his own purpose" (Prov. [16:4]), which is to say for his own glory "the Lord has worked"; and (4.2) for the benefit of mankind: "[Lest you raise your eyes to heaven and see the sun and moon, and all the stars of heaven, and led into error you adore them, and you worship] what the Lord your God made [as a service to all the peoples under heaven] (Deut. [4:19]). We should, therefore, use things for the glory of God, in order that we might please God in so doing. Similarly, you should use things for your own benefit, but not use them in opposition to God, as do sins: "All things are yours, and what from your hand [we have received, we have given back to you]" (1 Paralipomenon [29:14]).[12] Therefore whatsoever the knowledge, or riches, or beauty, you ought to point it all back and use it for the glory of God.

(5) We are led to a knowledge of human dignity. God made everything for humanity, as it is said in the Psalm: "[You have made him little less than the angels]. . . . All things you have subjected under his feet" [8:6–8]. After the angels, humanity is the most like God among all creatures. Thus we read: "Let us make men and women [to our own image and likeness]" and so forth [Gen. 1:26]. God did not say this about the heavens or the stars, but about human beings, and not as body but as incorruptible soul, having free will, by which they are more comparable to God than any other creature. Thus we ought to consider humanity to be more worthy than the rest of creation after the angels. We ought not in any way diminish our dignity either because of sin or because of an inordinate appetite for bodily things which are for our use and made for our service. By the same token we should consider ourselves as God made us, because God made human beings that they might surpass everything which lives on earth, and that they might be subject to God. Therefore we ought to have dominion and preeminence over things, and be in submission, in obedience, and in service toward God. Consequently we will attain the enjoyment of God, for which [let us pray], and so forth.

IV

This division of the Aquinas commentary concerns the meaning of Jesus Christ as the Son of God. Aquinas's review of the errors in the theological understanding of Jesus Christ, both truly God and truly human, is comprehensive and yet succinct. At issue in this commentary is the reality of the supernatural destiny of humankind. If Jesus is just a human being, no matter how great and good, then our destiny does not exceed the lot of human beings as creatures of God. If Jesus is God with us, then we are with Jesus in the destiny that he was given at the right hand of the Father.

At the end of the commentary there is an extraordinary and lovely exposition of Mary as symbol of the Christian, and as symbol of church, recapitulating the inner meaning of the incarnation. Accordingly, every Christian must hear, believe, meditate upon, communicate to others, and put into practice the word of God, so that it may become flesh in the church. Mary first harkens to the word of God, believes in God's word, then conceives God's word in her body, gives birth to the word of God made flesh, and finally nourishes that word by her self-giving way of life with others.

Et in Ihesum Christum Filius eius unicum, Dominum nostrum.

Non solum necesse est christiano credere esse unum Deum, et hunc creatorem celi et terre et omnium, sed etiam necessarium est ut credat quod Deus sit Pater et quod Christus sit uerus Filius Dei. Hoc autem, sicut dicit Petrus in canonica sua, non est fabulosum sed certum, et probat per uocem Dei in monte, dicens "Non enim indoctas fabulas secuti" etc., "in monte" etc. Ipse etiam Christus in pluribus locis uocauit Deum patrem suum et se dixit Filium Dei. Et ideo apostoli et sancti patres inter articulos fidei posuerunt quod Christus est Filius Dei, dicentes 'Et in Ihesum Christum Filium eius', scilicet Dei, supple 'Credo'.

Sed aliqui heretici fuerunt qui hoc peruerse crediderunt. Fotinus enim dixit quod Christus non est aliter filius Dei quam alii boni uiri, qui bene uiuendo merentur dici filii Dei per adoptionem, faciendo Dei uoluntatem; et ita Christus qui bene uixit et fecit Dei uoluntatem, meruit dici Filius Dei. Et uoluit quod Christus non fuerit ante beatam Virginem, sed tunc incepit quando ex ea conceptus est. Et sic in duobus errauit: in hoc quod non dixit eum uerum Filium Dei secundum naturam, et quod dixit eum secundum totum esse suum ex tempore fuisse; cum fides uera teneat quod sit Filius Dei per naturam et quod ab eterno sit, ac etiam habeamus expressas auctoritates in sacra Scriptura contra eum.

Nam contra primum dicitur quod sit non solum Filius Dei sed unigenitus, Io. "Vnigenitus qui est in sinu Patris, ipse nobis" etc. Contra secundum dicitur in Io. "Antequam Abraham fieret" etc.; constat autem quod Abraham fuit ante beatam Virginem. Et ideo sancti patres

And in Jesus Christ, his only Son, our Lord.

Not only must Christians believe there is one God, who is creator of heaven and earth and all things, but they must also believe that God is the Father, and Christ is the very Son of God. Peter argues in his canonical letter that this is not fiction but fact; it is proven through the voice of God on the mountain, saying: "Not following uneducated myths [have we made known to you the power and presence of our Lord, Jesus Christ; rather we were made eyewitnesses of that brilliance]" and so forth (2 Pet 1:16) "on the mountain" and so forth. Christ himself in several places called God his father and spoke of himself as Son of God. Therefore the apostles and holy fathers [of the church] placed among the articles of faith that Christ is the Son of God: "And in Jesus Christ, his Son," that is, God's son, and prefaced by "I believe."

There were some heretics, however, who believed this in a twisted way. Photinus[13] said that Christ is not otherwise the son of God than any other good man who by living well might merit to be called son of God through adoption, because of doing the will of God. And thus Christ, who lived well and did the will of God, merited to be called the son of God. Photinus opined that Christ did not exist before the blessed Virgin, but he began to exist when he was conceived by her. Thereby Photinus falls into two errors: (1) he does not speak of Christ as true Son of God by nature, and (2) he does speak of Christ as existing in time in all of his being. True faith, however, holds that he [Christ] is Son of God by nature, and that he is from all eternity. We also can produce explicit authority against Photinus in sacred Scripture.

In opposition to the first point, let it be said that Christ is not only Son of God, but only-begotten Son: "[No one has ever seen God;] the only-begotten Son, who is in the bosom of the Father, he [has told of him] to us" and so forth (John [1:18]). In opposition to the second point, let it be said, following John: "Before Abraham was, [I am]" and so forth [8:58]. But it is a fact that Abraham was before the blessed Virgin. And therefore the holy fathers [of the church] added in an-

addiderunt in alio symbolo, contra primum 'Filium Dei unigenitum', contra secundum 'ex Patre natum ante omnia secula'.

Sabellius uero, licet dixerit quod Christus fuerit ante beatam Virginem, tamen dixit quod non est alia persona Patris et alia Filii, sed ipse Pater est incarnatus, et ideo eadem persona est Patris et Filii. Sed hoc est erroneum, quia aufert trinitatem personarum; et contra hoc est auctoritas, Io. "Qui me misit uerax est" etc.; constat autem nullum a se mitti. Sic ergo mentitur Sabellius; et ideo in symbolo additur 'Deum de Deo, lumen de lumine', quasi Deum Filium de Deo Patre, et Filium qui est lumen de lumine Patre.

Arrius autem, licet diceret quod Christus fuerit ante beatam Virginem, et quod fuerit alia persona Patris et Filii, attribuit tamen tria Christo. Primum est quod fuit creatura; secundum est quod non fuerit ab eterno, sed in tempore factus a Deo nobilissima creatura; tertium est quod non fuerit unius nature Filius cum Deo Patre, et quod non fuerit uerus Deus. Quod similiter erroneum est, et est contra auctoritatem sacre Scripture. Dicitur enim in Io. "Ego et Pater unum sumus", scilicet in natura; et ideo sicut Pater fuit semper, ita et Filius. Et ideo in symbolo additum est 'Deum uerum de Deo uero', contra hoc quod dicit eum creaturam; 'genitum non factum', contra hoc quod dicit eum non fuisse ab eterno; 'consubstantialem Patri', contra hoc quod dicit eum non esse unuius nature cum Patre.

Patet ergo quod credere debemus quod Christus est uerus et unigenitus Filius Dei, et quod semper fuit cum Patre, et quod alia persona Filii et alia Patris, et in una natura cum Patre. Et si credimus hic per fidem, cognoscemus ea per perfectam uisionem in uita eterna; et ideo ad consolationem et edificationem aliquid dicamus de hiis.

Sciendum est autem quod diuersa diuersum generationis modum habent. Generatio autem Dei aliter est quam generatio aliarum rerum; et ideo non possumus ad aliquid pertingere de generatione Dei, nisi per generationem eius quod in creaturis magis accedit ad similitudinem Dei. Nichil est autem Deo ita simile sicut anima hominis,

other symbol [the Nicene Creed] in opposition to the first point, "the only-begotten Son of God," and in opposition to the second, "born of the Father before all ages."

Sabellius,[14] however, although he says that Christ existed before the blessed Virgin, nonetheless he does not speak of one person of the Father and another of the Son, but the Father himself has become incarnate. Therefore the same person is the Father and the Son. But this is in error, because it undoes the trinity of persons. In opposition is the authority of John: "[And if I myself judge, my judgment] is true, [because I am not alone, but I and the Father] who sent me" [8:16]. It is a fact, however, that no one sends himself. Thus Sabellius does not speak the truth, and therefore in the [Nicene] creed there is added: "God from God, light from light," as if God the Son is from God the Father, and the Son who is light is from the Father who is light.

Arius,[15] however, although he would say that Christ existed before the blessed Virgin, and that the Father and Son are not the same person, nonetheless attributes three notes to Christ: (1) that he was a creature; (2) that he was not from all eternity, but in time was made by God the most noble creature; (3) that the Son was not of one nature with God the Father, and that the Son was not true God. All this is equally in error, and is opposed to the authority of holy Scripture. We read in John: "I and the Father are one" [10:30], namely in nature. Therefore, just as the Father always existed, just so the Son. And thus, in opposition to speaking of Christ as a creature, the [Nicene] symbol adds: "true God from true God." In opposition to speaking of Christ as not being from all eternity, the symbol adds: "begotten not made." In opposition to speaking of Christ as not being of one nature with the Father, the symbol adds: "one in being with the Father."[16]

It is evident, therefore, that we ought to believe that Christ is the true and only-begotten Son of God, that he was always with the Father, and that the Father is one person and the Son another person, one in nature with the Father. If we believe these things through faith here and now, we shall know them through a perfect vision in life eternal. But for our consolation and edification let us say something further about them.

It is well-known that different beings have different ways of generation. The generation of God, however, is quite different from the generation of other things. However, we are not able to grasp the generation of God except through the generation of whatever in created things suggests a comparison with God. But nothing is so like God as the soul of a human being, as the saying goes. The way of

ut dictum est. Modus autem generationis in anima est quia homo per animam suam cogitat aliquid quod uocatur conceptio intellectus; et huiusmodi conceptus oritur ex anima sicut ex patre, et uocatur uerbum intellectus seu hominis. Anima igitur cogitando generat uerbum suum.

Sic et Filius Dei nichil aliud est quam Verbum Dei, non uerbum exterius prolatum, quia illud transit, sed uerbum interius conceptum; et ideo ipsum Verbum Dei est Filius Dei et unius nature et equalis Deo. Vnde et beatus Iohannes de Verbo loquens tres hereses destruxit: primo heresim Fotini que tacta est, et hoc cum dicit "In principio erat Verbum"; secundo Sabellii, dicens "et Verbum erat apud Deum"; tertio Arrii, cum dicit "et Deus erat Verbum".

Verbum autem aliter est in nobis et aliter est in Deo. In nobis enim uerbum nostrum est accidens; sed in Deo Verbum Dei idem est quod Deus, cum nichil sit in Deo quod non sit essentia Dei. Nullus autem potest dicere quod Deus non habeat Verbum, quia contingeret Deum esse insipientissimum; et ideo sicut semper fuit Deus, ita et Verbum eius. Sicut autem artifex omnia facit per formam quam primo in corde excogitat, que est uerbum eius, ita et Deus omnia facit Verbo suo, Io. i "Omnia per ipsum facta sunt" etc.

Si ergo Verbum Dei est Filius Dei, et omnia uerba Dei sunt similitudo quedam istius Verbi, debemus libenter audire uerba Dei: hoc enim est signum quod diligimus Deum, si libenter uerba eius audimus. Secundo, quod credamus uerba Dei, quia ex hoc Verbum Dei, scilicet Christus, habitat in nobis: Apostolus "Habitare Christum per fidem" etc.; Io. "Verbum Dei non habetis in uobis manens" etc. Tertio oportet quod Verbum Dei in nobis manens continue meditemus, quia non solum uerbum oportet credere sed et meditari, alias non prodesset. Et huiusmodi meditatio multum ualet contra peccata, Ps. "In corde meo abscondi eloquia tua" etc.; et in Psalmis de uiro iusto dicitur "In

generation in the soul is as follows. Through the soul a human being thinks something, which is called a concept of the intellect. A concept of this sort issues from the soul as from a father and is called an intellectual or human word. The soul, therefore, by thinking generates its own word.

Thus it is that the Son of God is nothing other than the Word of God, not a word expressed exteriorly, because such a word does not endure, but a word conceived interiorly. Therefore, the very Word of God is the Son of God, of one nature, and the same as God. Whence blessed John speaking of the Word destroys three heresies: (1) the heresy of Photinus mentioned earlier, when John says: "In the beginning was the Word"; (2) the heresy of Sabellius when John says: "and the Word was with God"; (3) the heresy of Arius, when John says: "and the Word was God" [all quotations from the Preface of John's Gospel].

The word, however, comes about in us in one way and in God in another way. The word in us is an "accident,"[17] whereas in God the Word of God is the same being as God, since nothing is in God that is not the essence of God. Nobody can say that God does not have a Word, because that would suggest God is without insight. Therefore, just as God always was, so his Word always was. Just as artisans make everything from a model that first they design in their heart, and that is their word, similarly God makes everything through God's own Word: "All things were made through him [and without him nothing was made that was made]" and so forth (John 1:[3]).

(1) Therefore, if the Word of God is the Son of God, and all the words of God resemble this Word, we ought to hear the words of God willingly. If we willingly hear his words, that is a sign we love God.

(2) Let us believe the words of God because in so doing the Word of God, namely Christ, dwells in us: "Christ to dwell through faith [in your hearts, that rooted and founded in charity, you might be able to understand with all the saints what might be the breadth and length, the height and the depth, and to know the love of Christ surpassing all knowledge, that you may be filled with the fullness of God]" and so forth (Paul [Eph. 3:17–18]). "And you will not have the Word of God abiding in you" and so forth (John [5:38]).

(3) It is necessary that we meditate upon the Word of God that continually abides in us, because it is necessary not only to believe the word but also to ponder it, otherwise it will not profit us. Meditation of this sort works very well against sin: "In my heart I enclosed your spoken words, [so that I might not sin]" and so forth (Ps. [118:11]). And in the Psalms we read of the just man: "[But his heart is in the law of the Lord] and in the law of the Lord I will meditate [day and

lege Domini meditabitur" etc. Vnde et beata Virgo "conseruabat omnia uerba hec" etc.

Quarto, quod homo manifestet uerbum Dei aliis. Cum enim cor hominis est plenum uerbo Dei, tunc debet effundere in alios predicando, ammonendo, inflammando. Eph. iv "Omnis sermo malus de ore uestro non procedat, sed si quis loquitur" etc. Et idem "Verbum Dei habitet in uobis habundanter".

Quinto uero uerbum Dei debet executioni demandari, Iac. "Estote factores uerbi" etc. Ista quinque seruauit per ordinem beata Virgo in generatione Verbi Dei ex se: primo audiuit, "Spiritus sanctus superueniet" etc.; secundo consensit per fidem, "Ecce ancilla Domini" etc.; tertio retinuit et portauit in utero; quarto protulit "et peperit filium suum primogenitum"; quinto nutriuit et lactauit, unde 'Sola Virgo lactabat' etc.

night]" and so forth [1:2]. Thus of the blessed Virgin we read: "[And his mother] treasured all these words [in her heart]" and so forth [Luke 2:51].

(4) So that we might manifest the word of God to others. When one's heart is full of the word of God, then it ought to overflow in preaching, counseling, and enkindling others: "May no bad speech come from your mouth, but if anyone speaks [may it be good speech for the edification of the faith that grace might be given to those who hear it]" (Eph. 4:[29]). Similarly, "May the Word of God dwell in you abundantly, [teaching in all wisdom, and admonishing one another with psalms, hymns, and spiritual canticles, singing thanks to God in your hearts]" [Col. 3:16].

(5) The word of God demands action indeed: "Be doers of the word, [and not only hearers, deceiving themselves]" and so forth (James [1:22]). These five considerations given above, the blessed Virgin kept in order in the generation of the Word of God from her: (1) she heard, "the Holy Spirit will overshadow" and so forth [Luke 1:35]; (2) she consented through faith, "Behold the handmaid of the Lord" and so forth [Luke 1:38]; (3) she kept the word and carried it in her womb; (4) she brought the Word forth, "she brought forth her first-born son" [Luke 2:7]; (5) she nourished the Word and nursed it, whence "Only a Virgin nursed"[18] and so forth.

V

This division of the Aquinas commentary concerns the enflesh-
ment of the Son of God, conceived by the Spirit but born of a woman.
Aquinas identifies several categories of wrong theological thinking
about the relationship of Jesus and Mary. (1) If Jesus has only an apparent body, then Mary is but a channel or surrogate mother through
whom God makes an appearance in this world. (2) If Jesus is a demi-
god, part human and part divine, then Mary is mother only of the
body of Jesus, but not of the human being Jesus. (3) If Jesus is a super-
man, but only a man nonetheless, then Mary is mother of only the
greatest of the sons of God. She is not mother of God.

Aquinas defends Mary as theotokos, truly mother of God. Jesus is the self-expression of God in human flesh; Jesus is the self-gift
of God.

In a succinct way, Aquinas lists the benefits to us of the incarnate Word of God: Christ knows God (faith); Christ became human
for our sake (hope); God so loved the world he gave his only Son
(love); as a temple of God we should not sin (moral life); and as
brother and sister of Christ we shall be with him where he now
reigns (eternal life).

── V

Qui conceptus est de Spiritu Sancto, natus ex Maria Virgine. Non solum est necessarium christiano credere Filium Dei, ut in precedentibus est ostensum, sed etiam oportet credere eius incarnationem. Et ideo beatus Iohannes, postquam dixerat de Verbo Dei multa subtilia et ardua, conuenienter nobis insinuauit eius incarnationem, cum dixit "Verbum caro factum est et habitauit in nobis". Et ut de hoc aliquid capere possitis, duo exempla ponam in medium.

Constat enim quod Filio Dei nichil est ita simile sicut uerbum in corde nostro conceptum, non prolatum. Nullus autem cognoscit uerbum dum est in corde hominis, nisi ille qui concipit; sed tunc primo cognoscitur cum profertur. Sic Verbum Dei, dum erat in corde Patris, non cognoscebatur nisi a Patre tantum; sed indutum carne tunc primo manifestum est et cognitum. Baruc "Post hoc in terris uisus est" etc.

Aliud exemplum est quia, licet uerbum prolatum cognoscatur per auditum, tamen non uidetur nec tangitur; sed cum scribitur in carta, tunc uidetur et tangitur. Sic et Verbum Dei uisibile et tangibile factum est, cum in carne uera fuit quasi scriptum; et sicut carta in qua scribitur uerbum regis dicitur uerbum regis, ita homo in quo est Verbum Dei dicitur Filius Dei. Ysa. "Sume tibi librum grandem et scribe in eo" etc. Et ideo apostoli sancti dixerunt 'Qui conceptus est de Spiritu Sancto, natus ex Maria Virgine'.

In quo quidem multi errauerunt; unde et sancti patres addiderunt in alio symbolo, in Nicena synodo, multa per que omnes illi errores destruuntur. Origenes dixit quod Christus ad hoc natus est et uenit in mundum ut saluaret etiam demones; et dixit demones esse saluandos omnes in fine mundi. Sed hoc est contra sacram Scripturam: dicitur enim Matth. "Ite maledicti" etc. Et ideo ad tollendum hunc er-

— V —

Who is conceived by the Holy Spirit, born of the Virgin Mary. It is necessary for a Christian not only to believe in the Son of God, as shown in the preceding, but also one must believe in his incarnation. Therefore blessed John, after he had written many nuanced and demanding insights about the Word of God, appropriately suggests his incarnation when he says: "The Word was made flesh and dwelt among us" [1:14]. And that the reader might grasp something from this, I will highlight two comparisons.

(1) Let us grant that the Son of God resembles nothing so much as the word conceived in our heart, but not expressed. No one, however, knows the word while it remains in the human heart, but the one who conceived it. It is then first known when it is expressed. Similarly, the Word of God, while in the heart of the Father, was not known except by the Father alone. But, then clothed with flesh, the Word is first made manifest and known: "After this he was seen on earth, and he conversed with human beings" and so forth (Bar. [3:38]).

(2) Another example. Although the expressed word is known through hearing, nonetheless it is not seen nor touched. When it is written on paper, however, then it is seen and touched. Similarly, the Word of God is made visible and palpable, when written as it were in real flesh. Just as the paper on which the word of the king is written is called the word of the king, so the one in whom the Word of God is [written] is called the Son of God: "Take up a great book, and write in it [in the style of humankind]" and so forth (Is. [8:1]). And therefore the holy apostles said [in the creed]: "Who was conceived by the Holy Spirit, born of the Virgin Mary."

In this matter many people have erred. Thus the holy fathers added in the other symbol, in the Nicene council, many phrases through which all these errors were overcome. Origen[19] said that Christ was born for this reason and came into the world that he might also save the demons. Origen said that all of the demons would be saved at the end of the world. But this is opposed to sacred Scripture, for Matthew says: "[Then he said to those on his left]: 'Depart from me, you wicked ones, [into eternal fire, which has been prepared for

57

rorem addiderunt 'Qui propter nos homines', non propter demones, 'et propter nostram salutem': in quo quidem apparet amor Dei ad nos.

Fotinus uero uoluit quod Christus natus est de Virgine, sed addidit quod esset purus homo; sed tamen bene uiuendo et faciendo Dei uoluntatem, meruit fieri filius Dei sicut et alii sancti uiri. Sed hoc est contra Domini auctoritatem in Io. "Descendi de celo non ut faciam uoluntatem meam" etc. Constat quod non descendisset de celo nisi fuisset ibi; et si fuisset purus homo, non fuisset in celo. Et ideo ad hoc remouendum addiderunt 'Descendit de celo'.

Manicheus dixit quod, licet Filius Dei fuerit semper et descenderit de celo, tamen non habuit ueram carnem, sed apparentem. Sed hoc est falsum; non enim decebat doctorem ueritatis aliquam falsitatem habere; et ideo sicut ostendit ueram carnem, sic habuit. Vnde et ipse dixit discipulis, Luc. "Palpate et uidete" etc. Et ideo ad hunc errorem remouendum addiderunt 'Et incarnatus est'.

Ebyon uero, quidam genere iudeus, dixit quod Christus natus est de beata Virgine, sed ex commixtione uiri et semine uirili. Sed hoc est falsum, quia angelus dixit "Quod enim in ea natum est" etc.; et sancti ad hoc remouendum addiderunt 'de Spiritu Sancto'.

Valentinus autem, licet confiteretur quod Christus fuerit conceptus de Spiritu Sancto, uoluit tamen quod Spiritus portauerit unum corpus celeste et posuerit in beata Virgine, et fuit corpus Christi; unde nichil operata est beata Virgo nisi quod fuit locus eius: unde dicebat quod ita transibat illud corpus per beatam Virginem sicut per aqueductum. Sed hoc est error, nam angelus dixit "Quod ex te nascetur sanctum" etc.; et ad Gal. "At ubi uenit plenitudo" etc., "factum ex muliere" etc. Et ideo addiderunt 'Natus ex Maria'.

Arrius autem et Appollinarius dixerunt quod, licet Christus sit Verbum Dei et natus ex Maria Virgine, tamen non habuit animam, sed loco anime fuit ibi diuinitas. Sed hoc est contra Scripturam, quia

the devil and his angels]'" and so forth [25:41]. And thus to remove this error they [the holy fathers] added [in the Nicene creed] "Who on account of us all," not on account of demons, "and on account of our salvation," in which indeed the love of God for us emerges.

Photinus maintained that Christ was indeed born of the Virgin, but he added that he was merely a man; nonetheless, by living well and doing the will of God, he merited to become a son of God just as other holy men. But this position is opposed to the authority of the Lord in John: "I came down from heaven not that I might do my own will, [but the will of him who sent me]" [6:38]. It is a fact that he would not have come down from heaven unless he would have been there. If he was merely a man, he would not have been in heaven. And so to overcome this position [of Photinus] they [the Nicene council fathers] added, "He came down from heaven."

Manicheus[20] said this: Although the Son of God always was and came down from heaven, nevertheless he did not have real flesh, but apparent flesh. But this is false, for it is unseemly for the teacher of the truth to have any falsity. Therefore he had real flesh just as he appeared to have. Thus Jesus himself said to the disciples: "Touch and see, [for a spirit does not have flesh and bones, as you see that I have]" (Luke [24:39]). And so to overcome this position [of Manicheus] they [the Nicene council fathers] added, "And was enfleshed."

Ebion,[21] however, who was of the Jewish race, said that Christ was born of the blessed Virgin, but by male seed from the intercourse of a man. But this is false, because the angel said: "For what is born in her [is by the Holy Spirit]" and so forth [Mt. 1:20]. And so to overcome this position [of Ebion] the holy fathers [of the Nicene council] added, "by the Holy Spirit."

Valentinus,[22] however, although he confessed that Christ was conceived by the Holy Spirit, nonetheless maintained that the Spirit transported a heavenly body and placed it in the blessed Virgin, and that became the body of Christ. Consequently, the blessed Virgin contributed nothing except a place for him. Thus it was said that the body of Christ passed through the blessed Virgin as through a conduit. But this is in error, for the angel said: "From you will be born the holy one" and so forth [Luke 1:35]; and in Galatians: "And when the fullness of time came, [God sent his own Son,] born of a woman," and so forth [4:4]. And therefore they [the Nicene council fathers] added, "born of Mary."

Arius and Apollinarius[23] both said that although Christ is the Word of God and born of the Virgin Mary, nonetheless he did not have a soul, but the divinity was there in place of the soul. But this

Christus dicit, Io. "Anima mea turbata est", et Matth. "Tristis est anima mea". Et ideo sancti ad remouendum hunc errorem addiderunt 'Et homo factus est'; homo enim ex anima et corpore constat, unde uerissime habuit omnia que uerus homo habet preter peccatum.

In hoc autem quod dicitur 'Et homo factus est', destruuntur omnes errores superius positi et omnes alii qui dici possent. Et precipue error Euticetis qui dixit commixtionem factam, scilicet ex natura diuina et humana factam, unam naturam Christi que nec Deus nec pure homo esset. Et hoc falsum est, quia tunc non esset homo; et esset contra hoc quod dicitur 'Et homo factus est'.

Destruitur etiam error Nestorii, qui dixit Filium Dei iunctum homini solum per inhabitationem; sed hoc est falsum, quia tunc non esset homo, sed in homine; et quod sit homo patet, Phil.ii "Habitu inuentus ut homo", Io.viii "Quid me queritis interficere", "hominem" etc.

Possumus autem ex hiis sumere aliqua ad eruditionem uite nostre. Primo enim ex hiis confirmatur fides nostra. Si enim aliquis diceret aliquid de aliqua terra remota et ipse non fuisset ibi, non ita crederetur ei sicut si fuisset. Ante uero quam Christus uenisset in mundum, patriarche, prophete, Iohannes Baptista dixerunt aliqua nobis de Deo; sed tamen non ita crediderunt eis homines sicut Christo qui uenit cum Deo, immo unum cum ipso. Vnde multum est firma fides ab ipso Christo tradita nobis, Io. "Deum nemo uidit umquam, unigenitus autem" etc. Et inde est quod multa secreta fidei manifesta sunt nobis post aduentum Christi, que ante occulta erant.

Secundo, ex hiis eleuatur spes nostra. Constat enim quod Christus Filius Dei non pro paruo ad nos uenit et sumpsit carnem nostram, sed pro magna utilitate nostra; unde fecit quoddam commercium, scilicet quod assumpsit animatum corpus de Virgine et nasci dignatus est, ut nobis suam diuinitatem largiretur. Et sic factus est homo ut hominem faceret Deum: Ro. "Iustificati igitur ex fide" etc., "per quem accessum habemus" etc.

is opposed to Scripture, because Christ said: "My soul is troubled" (John [12:27]), and "My soul is sad [even unto death]" (Mt. [26:38]). And so to overcome this error [of Arius and Apollinarius] the holy fathers [of the Nicene council] added, "And was made man." A man, however, consists of body and soul, and thus Christ would most genuinely have everything that a genuine man has, except sin.

In that phrase, "And was made man," all the errors listed above are overcome, as well as all other errors that might be voiced. In particular the error of Eutyches[24] is overcome, who said Christ was made by a commingling, partly from divine nature and partly from human, into a single nature that was neither God nor merely human. But this is wrong, because then he would not be human. And in opposition to this is said: "And was made man" [a human being].

The error of Nestorius[25] is also overcome, who said the Son of God was joined to the human through indwelling alone. But this is wrong, because then he would not be a human being, but in a human being. That he [Christ] is human is evident: [But he emptied himself, accepting the form of a servant, made in the likeness of humankind], found in a human condition" (Phil. 2:[7]); "Why do you seek to kill [me], a human being [who spoke the truth to you, which I heard from God]" (John 8:[40]).

We can gather some insights for the instruction of our own lives from the disputes above. (1) Our faith is confirmed from these. If anyone were to say something about any distant land, and they themselves had not been there, they would not be believed as though they had been. Yet, before Christ came into the world, the patriarchs, prophets, and John the Baptist spoke to us of the things of God. Nonetheless, we do not believe these people in the same way as we believe Christ, who came in the company of God and moreover was one with God himself. Thus the faith handed down to us from Christ himself is quite strong: "No one has ever seen God; but the only-begotten Son, [who is in the bosom of the Father, he has given an account]" and so forth (John [1:18]). And thus it is that many secrets of the faith, which previously were hidden, are made manifest to us after the coming of Christ.

(2) Our hope is raised from these considerations. Let us grant that Christ the Son of God came to us and assumed our flesh, not for a small but a great benefit to us. That is why he accomplished such an exchange, assuming a living body from the Virgin and consenting to be born, so that he might lavish his divinity upon us. Christ thus became man so that he might make man God: "Justified therefore by faith [we have peace with God through our Lord Jesus Christ]"

Tertio, ex hoc accenditur caritas. Nullum enim est ita euidens diuine caritatis indicium quam quod Deus creator omnium factus est creatura, Dominus factus est seruus, Filius Dei factus est filius hominis: Io. "Sic Deus dilexit mundum" etc. Et ideo ad huiusmodi considerationem amor noster reaccendi debet ad Deum.

Quarto inducimur ad considerandum naturam nostram puram. In tantum enim fuit natura nobilitata et exaltata ex coniunctione ad Deum, quod fuerit ad consortium diuine persone suscepta; unde et angelus, post incarnationem Christi, noluit sustinere quod beatus Iohannes adoraret eum, quod ante sustinuerat etiam a maximis patriarchis. Et ideo homo exaltationis huius se dignificans debet dedignari uilificari per peccatum se et naturam suam; et ideo dicit beatus Petrus "Per quem nobis" bona donantur, ut "diuine consortes nature, fugientes" etc.

Quinto, ex hiis inflammatur desiderium nostrum ad perueniendum ad Christum. Si enim aliquis rex esset frater alicuius, et esset remotus ab eo, desideraret ille cuius frater est peruenire ad eum et esse cum eo; unde cum Christus est frater noster, debemus desiderare esse cum eo et coniungi sibi. Matth. "Vbicumque fuerit corpus" etc.; Apostolus "Desiderium habens dissolui" etc. Quod quidem desiderium crescit in nobis, considerando incarnationem Christi.

Rogemus Dominum etc.

and so forth "through whom we have access [through faith to that grace, in which we stand, and we glory in the hope of the glory of the sons of God]" and so forth (Rom. [5:1–2]).

(3) Charity is enkindled. There is no clearer sign of divine love than that God the creator of all things has been made a creature, that the Lord has been made a servant, and that the Son of God has been made the son of man: "For God so loved the world [that he would give his only-begotten Son, so that everyone who believed in him would not perish, but have life everlasting]" and so forth (John [3:16]). Thus, through considerations of this sort our love towards God ought to be again enkindled.

(4) We are drawn to consider our nature in and of itself. Insofar as it was a nature accepted for companionship with a divine person, it was a nature ennobled and exalted from its involvement with God. Thus it is that after the incarnation, an angel was unwilling to allow blessed John to adore him, which hitherto the angel had allowed even the great patriarchs. Therefore human beings, prizing themselves with the dignity of this exaltation, ought to disdain to make themselves and their nature vile by sin. Thus blessed Peter says: "By which" he has given "to us" good things "[enormous and precious promises, so that through them you may become] sharers of the divine nature, escaping [the corruption which is in this world because of concupiscence]" and so forth [2 Pet 1:4].

(5) Our desire to draw close to Christ is enkindled. If there were a king and his brother, who was far away from him, that brother would desire to draw near, and to be with the king. Since Christ is our brother, we should desire to be with him and to be together with him: "Wherever the body might be, [there the eagles will gather]" and so forth (Mt. [24:28]). And St. Paul: "Having the desire to be dissolved [and to be with Christ, which is by far the better thing]" and so forth [Phil. 1:23]. Surely this desire grows in us, as we ponder the incarnation of Christ.

Let us pray to the Lord, and so forth.

This division of the Aquinas commentary concerns the meaning of the passion and death of Jesus Christ. Aquinas supports a bodiless condition for Jesus after his death and prior to his resurrection.
The human soul in a bodiless interim condition remains a classical
theology, although there are difficulties with such an anthropology.
The Greeks championed immortality of the soul, but the Christian
tradition speaks only of resurrection of the body. While there is a
gap between Good Friday and Easter Sunday in our time frame, in
eternity there may well be no waiting for events to come.

Equally classical is the atonement theology of Aquinas, which
holds that the suffering of the cross was the price of the redemption
of the human race.

The position that Aquinas takes with regard to the Jews, who
are accused of being Christ-killers, remains problematical. Quite common in the theology of the Middle Ages, and arising in a context of
animosity between Jews and Christians, the anti-Semitic flavor of
the condemnation of the Jews would seem to be understandable but
not excusable. In the medieval world of Dante's Inferno the sinner
is so identified with his or her sin that the guilt and punishment
remain inseparable from the sinner's very being for all eternity. In
a similar way, the Jews were identified with the death of Jesus and
the infinite offense of the death of God. Few theologians today would
support such an identification of a particular act with the whole
being of a person, much less with the whole being of a race of people. To continue to lay the guilt upon the Jews, and not upon us all,
and to overlook the words of Jesus to "forgive them for they do not
know what they do," seems unconscionable.[26]

Passus sub Pontio Pilato, crucifixus, mortuus et sepultus.

Sicut necessarium est christiano quod credat incarnationem Filii Dei, ita necessarium est quod credat eius passionem et mortem; quia, sicut Gregorius dicit, "nichil nasci profuit nisi redimi profuisset". Hoc autem, scilicet quod Christus pro nobis est mortuus, ita est arduum quod uix potest intellectus noster illud capere; immo nullo modo cadit in intellectu nostro. Et hoc est quod Baruc dicit "Ego opus faciam in diebus uestris" etc.; tanta enim est gratia et amor ipsius ad nos, quod plus ipse fecit nobis quam nos possumus capere.

Non tamen debemus credere quod Christus ita sustinuerit mortem quod diuinitas mortua sit, sed quod humana natura in ipso mortua sit: non enim mortuus secundum quod erat Deus, sed secundum hoc quod erat homo. Et hoc patet per duo exempla.

Vnum est in nobis: constat enim quod homo cum moritur, in separatione anime a corpore non moritur anima, sed ipsa caro seu corpus; sic in morte Christi non est mortua diuinitas, sed natura humana.

Sed si Iudei non occiderunt diuinitatem, uidetur quod non magis peccauerunt quam si occidissent alium hominem. Ad hoc dicendum est quod, dato quod rex aliquis esset indutus una pulcra ueste, si quis ergo inquinaret uestem illam, tantum reatum incurreret ac si ipsum regem inquinasset; Iudei autem, licet non possent diuinitatem occidere, tamen humanam naturam a Christo assumptam occidentes, tantum puniti sunt ac si ipsam diuinitatem occidissent.

Item, sicut dictum est, Filius Dei est Verbum Dei; et Verbum Dei incarnatum est sicut uerbum regis scriptum in carta. Si ergo aliquis dilaniaret cartam regis, pro tanto haberetur ac si dilaniaret uerbum regis; et ideo pro tanto habetur peccatum Iudeorum ac si occidissent Verbum Dei.

Suffered under Pontius Pilate, was crucified, was dead, and was buried.

Just as it is necessary that Christians believe in the incarnation of the Son of God, so they must believe in his passion and death. As Gregory says: "Nothing was gained by being born unless we should have gained by being redeemed."[27] That Christ died for us remains so impenetrable that our intellect is scarcely able to comprehend it. Indeed, in no way does it fall within our understanding. And this is what Baruch says: "I will do a work in your days [a work which you will not believe, should anyone narrate it to you]" and so forth [Acts 13:41].[28] So great is the favor and love of Christ for us, that he does more for us than we can comprehend.

Nevertheless, we need not believe that Christ so underwent death that the divinity would be dead, but rather that human nature in him would be dead. He did not die insofar as he was God, but insofar as he was human. And this is clear from two illustrations.

(1) Take us for example. Let us grant that when a human being dies, the soul does not die in the separation of the soul from the body, but the flesh or the body itself dies. Similarly, in the death of Christ the divinity does not die, but the human nature.

(2) If the Jews, however, did not kill the divinity, it would seem that they did no more sin than if they had killed any human being. I would give this response. Let us suppose some king were dressed in a single beautiful garment and someone were to dirty that garment. That person would incur guilt proportionate to besmirching the king himself. Although the Jews were not able to kill the divinity, nevertheless in killing the human nature assumed by Christ, they are punished as much as if they had killed the divinity.[29]

Similarly, as it is said, the Son of God is the Word of God. And the Word of God has been enfleshed as the word of the king written on a paper. If anyone were to tear up the paper of the king, it would be considered just as seriously had they torn up the word of the king. Therefore the sin of the Jews is considered just as seriously had they killed the Word of God.

Sed que necessitas quod Filius Dei pateretur pro nobis? Magna. Et potest colligi duplex necessitas: una est ad remedium contra peccata, alia est ad exemplum quantum ad agenda. Ad remedium quidem, quia contra omnia mala que incurrimus propter peccata, inuenimus remedium per passionem Christi. Inuenimus autem per peccatum quinque.

Primo, maculam. Homo enim cum peccat, deturpat animam suam; quia, sicut uirtus anime est pulcritudo eius, ita peccatum est eius macula: Baruch "Quid est, Israel, quod in terra inimicorum es" etc., "inueterasti" etc., "deputatus es cum mortuis" etc. Sed hoc remouet passio Christi, nam Christus sua passione fecit balneum de sanguine suo, quo peccatores lauantur: Apoc. "Dilexit nos" etc. Lauatur autem anima sanguine Christi in baptismo, quia ex sanguine Christi habet uirtutem regeneratiuam. Et ideo cum quis se iterum per peccatum inquinat, facit iniuriam Christo et magis peccat quam ante: Hebr. "Irritam quis faciens legem Moysi" etc.; "duxerit" etc.

Secundo, incurrimus offensam Dei. Nam sicut homo corporalis diligit corporalem pulcritudinem, ita et Deus spiritualem que est pulcritudo anime; quando ergo anima per peccatum inquinatur, Deus offenditur et habet odio peccatorem: Sap. "Pariter est odio Deo impius et impietas sua". Sed hoc passio Christi remouet, qui Deo Patri satisfecit pro peccato hominis, pro quo homo ipse satisfacere non poterat; cuius caritas et obedientia maior fuit quam preuaricatio et peccatum hominis. Ro. "Cum inimici essemus, Deo reconciliati sumus" etc.

Tertio, incurrimus infirmitatem. Nam homo semel peccando credit postmodum continere a peccato; sed totum contrarium est, quia per unum peccatum debilitatur et fit pronior ad peccandum. Vnde cum primus homo peccauit, nostra natura fuit debilitata et corrupta, et ex tunc pronior ad peccandum; et peccatum est magis dominatiuum homini.

But, what was the necessity that the Son of God should suffer for us? Great need. And it can be reduced to necessity that is twofold. (1) A remedy against sin, and (2) an example for behavior. As for the "remedy," through the passion of Christ we find a remedy against all the evils that we undergo because of sin. We discover, however, five evils because of sin.

(1.1) Stain. When human beings sin, they soil their own soul, because as virtue of the soul is its beauty, so sin is its defilement: "How is it, O Israel, that you are in the land of your enemies" and so forth; "that you grow old [in an alien land, that you are defiled with the dead,] that you are put among the dead [those going down into hell?]" and so forth (Bar. [3:10–11]).³⁰ But the passion of Christ takes this away, for by his passion Christ makes a bath of his own blood, in which sinners are washed: "[And from Jesus Christ who is a faithful witness, the first-born of the dead, and the sovereign of the kings of the earth;] who loved us, [and washed us in his blood from our sins]" (Apoc. [1:5]). In baptism the soul is washed in the blood of Christ, because baptism is a rebirth in the blood of Christ. And therefore, whenever anyone defiles himself again through sin, he does an injury to Christ and sins more than before: "Anyone undoing the law of Moses, [given two or three witnesses, dies without any mercy]" and so forth. "[How much more severe punishment do you think he would merit who has trampled upon the Son of God, and] brought to [pollution the blood of the covenant, in which he was sanctified, and who gave insult to the spirit of grace?]" (Heb. [10:28–29]).

(1.2) We commit an offense against God. Just as a bodily human being loves bodily beauty, just so God loves spiritual beauty, which is beauty of soul. Therefore, when the soul is soiled through sin, God is offended and holds the sinner in aversion: "The impious and their impiety God likewise holds in aversion" (Wis. [14:9]). The passion of Christ undoes this. He made satisfaction to God the Father for the sin of humanity, for which human beings themselves were not able to make satisfaction. His love and obedience were greater than the divided heart and sin of humanity: "If when we were enemies we have been reconciled to God [through the death of his Son, how much the more now that we are reconciled will we be saved through his life]" and so forth (Rom. [5:10]).

(1.3) We undergo debilitation. Having once sinned, we believe afterwards we can control sin. Just the opposite, because through one sin we are weakened and made more prone to sinning. Thus when the first human sinned, our nature became weakened, corrupted, and then on more prone to sinning. And sin is yet more the tyrant over humanity.³¹

Sed Christus hanc debilitatem et infirmitatem licet non totum deleuerit, ita tamen ex passione Christi homo confortatus est et peccatum debilitatum, quod non tantum dominatur homini. Et homo potest conari, adiutus gratia Dei que confertur in sacramentis, que ex passione Christi habent efficaciam, quod potest resistere peccatis; et ideo dicit Apostolus Ro. "Vetus homo noster simul crucifixus est" etc. Et inde est quod ante passionem Christi pauci inuenti sunt sine peccato mortali uiuentes, sed post passionem eius multi qui sine peccato uixerunt.

Quarto, incurrimus reatum pene. Hoc enim exigit iustitia Dei, ut quicumque peccat puniatur; pena autem pensatur ex culpa. Vnde cum culpa peccati mortalis sit infinita, ut puta contra bonum infinitum, scilicet Deum, cuius precepta peccator contempnit, pena debita peccato mortali est infinita. Sed Christus per passionem suam abstulit nobis penam et sustinuit ipse: "Peccata nostra", id est penam pro peccatis, "pertulit in corpore suo" etc. Nam passio Christi fuit tante uirtutis quod suffecit ad expiandum omnia peccata totius mundi, et adhuc si essent centum. Et inde est quod baptizati ab omnibus peccatis mundantur; inde est etiam quod sacerdos omnia peccata dimittit. Inde est etiam quod quicumque se magis passioni conformat, maiorem consequitur ueniam et plus meretur de gratia.

Quinto, incurrimus exilium regni. Nam qui offendunt reges, exulari coguntur a regno; sic et homo per peccatum expellitur de paradiso: inde est quod post peccatum Adam statim eiectus est de paradiso, et clausa est ianua paradisi.

Sed Christus passione sua ianuam paradisi aperuit, et reuocauit exules ad regnum. Aperto enim latere Christi, aperta est ianua paradisi; et effuso sanguine eius deleta est macula, placatus est Deus, ablata est debilitas, expiata est pena, exules ad regnum reuocantur. Et inde est quod statim latroni dixit "Hodie mecum eris in paradiso". Hoc non dictum est olim, hoc non dictum est Ade, non Abrahe, non Dauid; sed hodie quando aperta est ianua, latro ueniam petit. Hebr. "Habemus fiduciam per sanguinem Christi" etc.

Although Christ did not totally put an end to this weakness and debilitation, nevertheless by the passion of Christ humanity is strengthened and sin is weakened to the extent that it does not further dominate humankind. Human beings can struggle, aided by the grace of God which is conferred in the sacraments. From the passion of Christ they have their efficacy, which is able to resist sin. Therefore Paul says: "Our old man was crucified with him [that we might destroy the body of sin, and no longer serve sin]" and so forth (Rom. [6:6]). Thus it is that before the passion of Christ, few people were found living without mortal sin, whereas after his passion many are found who live without sin.

(1.4) We undergo the consequences of wrongdoing. The justice of God demands that whoever sins be punished. The punishment, however, is proportioned to the guilt. Since the guilt of a mortal sin is infinite — considering it offends an infinite good, namely God, whose precepts the sinner spurns — the punishment due to mortal sin is infinite. But Christ through his passion took this punishment away from us and he himself suffered it: "Our sins" that is, the punishment for our sins, "he took into his own body [on the wood of the cross, that dead to sin we might live to justice]" and so forth [1 Pet 2:24]. Indeed the passion of Christ was of such great power that it sufficed for expiating the sins of the whole world, yes even a hundred worlds. Thus it is that the baptized are cleansed of all sins, and likewise that the priest forgives all sins. Consequently, whoever conform themselves more to the passion of Christ, the greater pardon follows and the more by grace is merited.

(1.5) We undergo exile from the kingdom [of God]. Those who offend kings are driven into exile away from the kingdom. Similarly, humanity is expelled from paradise because of sin. Thus it is that Adam was put out of paradise immediately after sinning, and the door of paradise was shut.

Christ, however, by his passion opened the door of paradise, and called the exiles back into the kingdom. Having opened the side of Christ [on the cross], the door of paradise was opened. Having poured out his blood, the stain [of sin] is removed, God is pleased, the weakness [of sin] is taken away, the punishment [due to sin] is lifted, and the exiles are called back to the kingdom. Thus it is that he [Jesus] said to the thief in an instant: "Today you will be with me in paradise" [Luke 23:43]. This was not said previously; this was not said to Adam, nor to Abraham, nor to David. Yet, today when the door [of the kingdom of God] is open, he [Jesus] offers pardon to the thief: "We have confidence through the blood of Christ, [brothers, in the access of the saints]" and so forth (Heb. [10:19]).

Sic ergo patet utilitas ex parte remedii. Sed non minor est utilitas quantum ad exemplum: nam, sicut dicit Augustinus, passio Christi sufficit ad informandum totaliter uitam nostram. Quicumque enim uult perfecte uiuere, nichil aliud faciat nisi ut contempnat que Christus contempsit, et appetat que Christus appetiit: nullum exemplum uirtutis abest a cruce.

Si enim exemplum queris caritatis, "maiorem caritatem nemo habet" etc.: hoc Christus in cruce. Et ideo si pro nobis dedit animam suam, non debet esse graue sustinere quecumque mala pro eo. Ps. "Quid retribuam Domino" etc.; "calicem" etc.

Si queris patientiam, excellentior in cruce inuenitur. Patientia enim ex duobus redditur magna: aut cum magna quis suffert patienter, aut cum ea suffert que uitare posset et non uitat. Sed Christus magna pertulit in cruce, Thren. "O uos omnes qui transitis" etc.; et patienter, quia "cum pateretur" etc.; Ysa. "tanquam ouis" etc. Item uitare potuit et non uitauit: Io. "An putas quoniam rogare possum Patrem" etc. Magna ergo est patientia Christi in cruce. Hebr. "Per patientiam curramus ad propositum nobis certamen" etc.; "confusione contempta" etc.

Si queris exemplum humilitatis, respice crucifixum. Nam Deus uoluit iudicari sub Pontio Pilato et mori: Ysa. "Causa tua quasi impii iudicata est"; uere 'quasi impii', quia "morte turpissima condempnemus eum", Sap. Dominus pro seruo et uita angelorum pro homine mori uoluit: Phil. "Factus obediens" Patri etc.

Si queris exemplum obedientie, sequaris eum qui factus est obediens: Ro. "Sicut enim per inobedientiam unius", scilicet Ade, "peccatores" etc.

(2) Thus it is clear how useful a remedy it [the passion of Christ] is, and no less useful an example. As Augustine says, the passion of Christ suffices for completely modeling our life.[32] Whosoever wishes to live with perfection should do nothing other than to despise what Christ despises, and desire what Christ desires. Not a single example of virtue is lacking from the [example of the] cross.

(2.1) If one seeks an example of love, "no one has any greater charity, [than the one who lays down his life for his friends]" and so forth [John 15:13]. This Christ does on the cross. And therefore if he gave his life for us, it ought not to be hard to put up with any evil whatsoever for him: "What will I give back to the Lord [for all the things which he has given to me]" and so forth; "[I will lift up the] cup [of salvation, and I will call upon the name of the Lord]" and so forth (Ps. [115:12–13]).

(2.2) If one seeks an example of patience, none more excellent than the cross will be found. Patience is considered great for two reasons: either when someone greatly suffers with patience, or when someone suffers what they might have avoided and did not. But Christ suffered greatly on the cross: "O all you who pass by [on the way, attend and see if there is a sorrow like my sorrow!]" and so forth (Lam. [1:12]). And [Christ suffered] with patience, because "when he suffered [he did not hurl threats]" and so forth [1 Pet 2:23]; and "as a sheep [he was led to the slaughter]" and so forth (Is. [53:7]). Similarly, [he suffered what] he might have avoided and did not: "Or do you think that I am [not] able to ask [my] Father, [and he would furnish me in an instant with more than twelve legions of angels]" and so forth (John [Mt. 26:53]). Great therefore is the patience of Christ on the cross: "In patience let us embrace the struggle put before us" and so forth, "[Jesus, who for the joy held out to him, endured the cross,] despising the shame" and so forth (Heb. [12:1–2]).

(2.3) If one seeks an example of humility, look upon the cross. God chose to be judged under Pontius Pilate and to be put to death: "As if your case was one of the wicked, it was judged" (Is. [Job 36:17]). "As if one of the wicked" because "I have been condemned to a most wretched death" (Wis. [2:20]). The Lord chose to die for a servant, and the life of angels for humankind: "[He humbled himself,] made obedient" to the Father ["unto death, even the death of the cross"] and so forth (Phil. [2:8]).

(2.4) If one seeks an example of obedience, you might follow him who was made obedient: "Just as through the disobedience of one human being" namely, Adam, "[many became] sinners, [so through the obedience of one, many became just]" and so forth (Rom. [5:19]).

Si queris exemplum contempnendi terrena, sequere eum[1] "in quo sunt omnes thesauri" etc., in cruce nudatum, delusum, consputum, cesum, spinis coronatum, et demum aceto et felle potatum. Non ergo afficiaris ad uestes et diuitias, quia "diuiserunt sibi uestimenta mea"; non ad honores, quia "ludibria et uerbera expertus"; non ad dignitates, quia "plectentes coronam spineam imposuerunt" capiti meo; non ad delicias, quia "in siti mea potauerunt me aceto".[2]

Rogemus Dominum.

(2.5) If one seeks an example of despising earthly things, follow him "in whom all the treasures [of wisdom and knowledge are hidden]" and so forth [Col. 2:3],³³ nude on the cross, made sport of, spat upon, bruised, crowned with thorns, and at the last given bitter and sour wine to drink. Therefore do not attach yourself to your clothes and riches, because "they divided my vestments among them" [Ps. 21:19 and in Mark 15:24], nor to honors, because "acquainted with mockeries and beatings" [Heb. 11:36], nor to especial dignity, because "twisting a crown of thorn they put it down" [John 19:2] on my head, nor to delights, because "in my thirst they gave me vinegar wine to drink" [Ps. 68:22].³⁴

Let us pray to the Lord.

This division of the Aquinas commentary concerns the meaning of Jesus' descent to the realm of the dead. In the deliverance that Jesus brings to those awaiting the kingdom of God, those who died in mortal sin are excluded. More controversial, however, would be the fate of those who remain in hell because they have died in original sin not taken away by explicit faith in an adult, or baptism in a child. The doctrine of limbo for unbaptized children comes out of such a consideration. If children could be saved without baptism, it would seem they were saved without grace. It was a dilemma common enough in the theology of the Middle Ages, although not given much credence today. While logically it would seem necessary to come to salvation either by explicit faith or by child baptism, such logic limits the infinite resourcefulness of the God who wishes to save everyone.

In the following section, Aquinas treats unbelievers as worthy of neither judgment nor condemnation. The Middle Ages simply did not know what to do with the unbeliever, either the child too young to believe or the adult who refused to embrace the faith.

Aquinas lists benefits of the descent into hell for those living. He puts fear of hell into balance with hope of heaven. There is an appeal to both punishment as a deterrent and reward as a motivator. He closes his commentary on the fifth article of the creed with an appeal to the Christian to pray for the souls in purgatory, in order to do for them what Jesus did in his descent into hell.

Descendit ad inferos.

Sicut dictum est, mors Christi fuit in separatione anime a corpore sicut et mors aliorum hominum; sed diuinitas sic indissolubiliter unita fuit homini Christo quod, licet anima et corpus separarentur ad inuicem, ipsa tamen diuinitas perfectissime affuit semper et anime et corpori. Et ideo in sepulcro cum corpore fuit Filius Dei, et ad infernum descendit cum anima; et ideo sancti apostoli dixerunt 'Descendit ad inferos'.

Sunt autem quatuor rationes quare Christus secundum animam ad inferna descendit. Prima ratio est ut sustineret totam penam peccati, et sic totam culpam expiaret. Pena autem peccati hominis non solum erat mors corporis, sed etiam erat in anima, quia etiam peccatum erat quantum ad animam; et ideo post mortem descendebant ad infernum ante aduentum Christi. Vt ergo Christus perfecte sustineret totam penam debitam peccatoribus, uoluit etiam non solum mori, sed ad infernum secundum animam descendere. Et ideo in Ps. "Estimatus sum cum descendentibus in lacum".

Aliter tamen Christus descendit ad inferos, et aliter antiqui patres; nam patres cum necessitate et sicut uiolenter ducti et detenti, Christus uero cum potestate et sponte. Et ideo sequitur in Ps. "Factus sum sicut homo sine adiutorio inter mortuos liber": alii enim erant ibi ut serui, sed Christus ut liber.

Secunda ratio est ut perfecte subueniret bonis omnibus et suis. Christus enim habebat suos non solum in mundo, sed etiam in inferno: in hoc enim aliqui sunt Christi in quantum habent caritatem. In inferno autem erant multi qui cum caritate et fide Venturi decesserant, sicut Abraham, Isaac, Iacob et Dauid, et alii iusti et perfecti uiri; et ideo quia Christus uisitauerat suos in mundo isto et subuenerat eis per mortem suam, uoluit etiam uisitare suos qui erant in

—— VII ——

He descended into hell.

As we say, the death of Christ lies in the separation of the soul from the body, just as in the death of other human beings. But, the divinity was so indissolubly united to the humanity of Christ that, although body and soul were separated from each other, nonetheless the very divinity was always perfectly present both to the soul and the body. Therefore, the Son of God was both in the tomb with the body and descended into hell with the soul. And thus the holy apostles said: "he descended into hell."

There are four reasons why Christ as a soul descended into hell. (1) To shoulder the full punishment of sin, and so expiate all of its guilt. The punishment of sin for humanity, however, was not only the death of the body, but also involved the soul, because sin also belonged to the soul. And thus before the coming of Christ, the soul after death descended into hell. In order that Christ completely shoulder the entire punishment due to sinners, he wished not only to die, but also to descend into hell as a soul. Thus we read: "I am labeled with those going down into the depths" (Ps. [87:5]).

Nonetheless, Christ descended into hell in one way, and the fathers of old in another. The ancient fathers were conducted and detained there from necessity, and as if violently, whereas Christ went down in power and on his own initiative. And therefore the Psalm above continues: "I am made like a man without help, yet free among the dead" [87:5–6]. The others [who were dead] were there as slaves, but Christ was there as a free man.

(2) So that he would completely rescue all good people [of past generations] and his own friends [who died in his lifetime]. Christ indeed had his own friends not only in the [upper] world, but also in the underworld. People were friends of Christ in the world insofar as they had charity. In the underworld, however, there were many people, such as Abraham, Isaac, Jacob, and David, and other just and virtuous men, who departed with charity and with faith in the One who was to come. And therefore just as Christ visited his own friends in this world and rescued them through his own death, so he wanted

inferno, et subuenire eis descendendo ad eos. Eccli. xxiiii "Penetrabo inferiores partes terre" etc.

Tertia ratio est ut perfecte triumpharet de dyabolo. Tunc enim perfecte aliquis triumphat contra aliquem, quando non solum uincit eum in campo, sed aufert ei sedem regni sui et domum suam. Christus autem triumphauerat contra dyabolum in cruce et uicerat eum, unde dixit "Nunc iudicium est mundi, nunc princeps huius mundi", id est dyabolus, "eicietur foras", scilicet de mundo; et ideo ut perfecte triumpharet, uoluit etiam ei auferre sedem regni sui, et ligare eum in domo sua que erat infernus. Et ideo descendit illuc et diripuit omnia sua; et ligauit eum et abstulit ei predam suam: Col. "Expolians principatus et potestates, transduxit confidenter" etc.

Similiter etiam quia iam Christus acceperat potestatem celi et terre, uoluit etiam possessionem inferni accipere, ut sic secundum Apostolum "In nomine Ihesu omne genu" etc.; Marci ultimo "In nomine meo demonia eicient".

Quarta ratio est ut liberaret sanctos qui erant in inferno. Christus enim sicut uoluit pati mortem ut liberaret uiuentes a morte, ita uoluit descendere ad infernum ut liberaret sanctos qui erant ibi ab inferno. Zac. "Tu autem in sanguine" etc.; Osee "Ero mors tua" etc. Licet enim mortem totaliter destrueret, infernum tamen non omnino destruxit sed momordit, quia non omnes liberauit ab inferno, sed illos tantum qui fuerunt sine peccato mortali: scilicet sine peccato originali, a quo quantum ad personam mundati erant per circumcisionem,[3] et sine actuali; sed erant ibi propter originale peccatum Ade, a quo quantum ad naturam non potuerunt liberari nisi per Christum. Et dimisit ibi illos qui fuerunt in peccato mortali, et pueros non baptizatos; et ideo dicit "Morsus tuus ero" etc.

Sic ergo patet quod Christus descendit ad inferos, et propter quid.

to visit his own who were in hell, and to rescue them by descending to them: "I will penetrate the deepest parts of the earth, [and I will look upon all those who have died, and I will enlighten all those hoping in God]" and so forth (Ecclus. 24:[45]).

(3) That he might completely triumph over the devil. Consider that someone perfectly triumphs over another when they not only conquer them in the open field but also snatch from them the heart of their own kingdom and their home. Christ, however, triumphed over the devil on the cross and he conquered him, whence he says "Now is the judgment of the world, now is the judgment of the prince of this world," that is, the devil, "and he will be tossed out," from the world [John 12:31]. Therefore, in order to triumph completely, Christ wanted also to capture the heart of the devil's kingdom, and to bind him in his own house, which was hell.[35] Christ thus went down there and plundered all his goods; he bound the devil and stripped from him his own spoils: "Undoing the principalities and powers, he disgraced [them] with ease" and so forth (Col. [2:15]).

Similarly, since Christ already had reigned sovereign in heaven and on earth, he wished also to assume possession over hell, as Paul says: "In the name of Jesus every knee [should bend of those in heaven, and on earth, and in hell]" and so forth [Phil. 2:10]. And in the last chapter of Mark we read: "[and these signs will follow those who believe]. In my name they will cast out demons" [16:17].

(4) That he might free the saints who were in hell. Just as Christ wished to suffer death that he might free from death those living, so he wished to descend into hell that he might free from hell the saints who were there: "As for you, in the blood [of the covenant, I will set free your captives from the dry depths]" (Zech. [9:11]). And in Hosea: "[From the hand of death I will free them, from death I will redeem them.] I will be your death, [O death! I will be your sting, O hell!]" and so forth [13:14]. Although Christ completely destroyed death, nonetheless he did not all together destroy hell. Rather, Christ stung hell, because he did not free everyone from hell, but only those who were without mortal sin, that is, without original sin (from which they are cleansed as individuals by circumcision) and without actual [mortal] sin. These souls were there on account of the original sin of Adam, from which they could not be freed by nature but only by Christ. But he sent away those who were there in mortal sin and children who were not baptized. Therefore it is said [in Hosea above]: "I will be your sting" and so forth.

It is clear therefore that Christ did descend into hell and why he did so.

Ex hiis possumus ad instructionem nostram accipere quatuor. Primo spem firmam de Deo: nam quantumcumque homo sit in afflictione, non debet desperare nec diffidere de adiutorio Dei. Nichil ita graue inuenitur sicut esse in inferno; si ergo Christus illos qui erant in inferno liberauit, multum debet quilibet confidere, si est amicus Dei, ut liberetur ab eo in quacumque sit tribulatione. Sap. "Hec", scilicet sapientia, "uenditum iustum non derelinquit, descenditque" etc. Et quia specialiter seruos suos iuuat Deus, multum debet esse securus ille qui seruit Deo. Sap. "Qui timet Deum non trepidabit".

Item, secundo debemus concipere timorem et presumptionem propellere. Christus enim, licet passus sit pro peccatoribus et descenderit ad inferos, non liberauit omnes sed illos tantum qui sine peccato erant, ut dictum est; illos uero qui in mortali decesserant dimisit. Et ideo nullus qui in peccato mortali decedit, debet sperare ueniam, sed tantum esse in inferno quantum sancti in paradiso, scilicet in perpetuum. Matth. "Ibunt hii in supplicium eternum, iusti autem" etc.

Item, tertio ex hoc concipimus sollicitudinem. Nam Christus secundum animam descendit ad inferos pro salute nostra; et nos frequenter debemus[4] descendere, considerando scilicet penas eternas: Ysa. "Ego dixi: In dimidio dierum meorum" etc. Qui enim frequenter per cogitationem descendit in uita, non de facili descendit in morte, quia consideratio huius retrahit a peccato. Videmus enim quod homines huius mundi cauent sibi a maleficiis propter penam temporalem; quanto magis debent cauere propter penam inferni, que maior est et quantum ad diuturnitatem et quantum ad acerbitatem. Eccli. "Memorare nouissima tua, et in eternum" etc.

Item, quarto prouenit ex hoc nobis exemplum dilectionis. Christus enim descendit ad inferos, ut liberaret suos qui erant ibi; unde et nos debemus illuc descendere, ut subueniamus nostris qui sunt ibi, ipsi enim nichil possunt; et ideo nos debemus subuenire eis qui sunt in purgatorio. Nimis enim esset durus, qui non subueniret amico suo qui esset in carcere; quanto ergo magis est durus, qui non succurrit amico qui est in purgatorio.[5] Iob "Miseremini mei" etc.; Eccli. "A

From these considerations we can draw four conclusions for our own instruction. (1) Firm hope in God. No matter how anyone may be in affliction, they should not despair nor lose trust in the assistance of God. Nothing can be found so dire as being in hell. If Christ freed those who were in hell, everyone ought to trust greatly, if they are a friend of God, that they will be freed by God no matter what may be the tribulation: "She," that is, wisdom, "did not abandon the just man when he was sold, but she went down [with him into the pit and freed him from sinners]" (Wis. [10:13]). And because God helps especially God's servants, anyone who serves God should be quite secure: "Anyone who fears God will not be alarmed, [and will not panic, because God is their hope]" (Wis. [Ecclus. 34:16]).

(2) We should become afraid [of hell] and drive away presumption. Although Christ suffered for sinners and did descend into hell, he nonetheless did not free everyone, but only those who were without [mortal] sin. As it is said: but those who died in mortal sin he sent away. Therefore, no one who dies in mortal sin should hope for pardon, but [should expect] to be in hell just as long as the saints are in paradise, that is to say, forever: "And those [on Christ's left hand] will go into eternal torment, [the just, however, into everlasting life]" and so forth (Mt. [25:46]).

(3) We should become careful. Christ descended as a soul into hell for our salvation, and hence we ought frequently to descend there by considering eternal punishment: "I said: in the middle of my days [I will go to the gates of hell]" and so forth (Is. [38:10]). Whoever frequently goes down to hell in thought during this life, will not go down there easily in death, because the consideration of hell draws one away from sin. We see how people in this world protect themselves against earthly pain from evildoers; how much more ought they to protect themselves against the pain of hell, which is greater in duration as well as in bitterness: "[And in all you do,] remember the end of your days, and for eternity [you will not sin]" and so forth (Ecclus. [7:40]).

(4) We are shown an example of love. Christ descended into hell in order to free those who were there. Consequently, we ought to go down to that place, that we might come to the aid of our own [friends] who are there, for they are not able to do anything. Therefore we should support those who are in purgatory. The man who would not come to the aid of his friend who was in prison would be thoroughly callous. How much more unfeeling the man who does not come to the aid of a friend who is in purgatory. "Have pity on me, [have pity on me at least you, my friends, because the hand of God has pressed upon me]" and so forth (Job [19:21]). And in Ecclesiasticus we read:

mortuo non subtrahas gratiam"; Mach. "Sancta ergo et salubris est" etc.

Subuenitur autem eis precipue per tria, sicut dicit Augustinus: per missas, per eleemosynas et per orationes; Gregorius addit quartum, scilicet per ieiunium. Nec est mirum, quia etiam in mundo isto potest amicus satisfacere pro amico; intelligendum est de illis qui sunt in purgatorio.

Rogemus.

"From the dead you will not withdraw grace" [7:37]. And in Maccabees: "Therefore it is a holy and beneficial [thought to pray for the dead, that they might be absolved from their sins]" and so forth [2 Mac. 12:46].

We come to their assistance principally in three ways, as Augustine[36] says: through masses, through almsgiving, and through prayers. Gregory[37] adds a fourth way, through fasting. We should not wonder, because even in the world one friend can make satisfaction for another. We should understand the same thing about those in purgatory.

Let us pray [to the Lord].

VIII

This division of the Aquinas commentary concerns the meaning of the resurrection. Aquinas lists distinguishing notes of the resurrection of Christ: (1) Jesus rises of his own power, since "no one takes his life"; (2) Jesus rises to die no more, unlike Lazarus; (3) Christ rises by his own power, whereas the Christian will rise through Christ; (4) Christ rises now, whereas the Christian will rise at the end. Significantly, Aquinas then argues that the Christian should repent now in order to rise then.

Tertia die resurrexit a mortuis.

Duo necessaria sunt homini ad cognoscendum, scilicet gloria Dei et pena inferni; nam per gloriam allecti et per penam territi, cauent sibi homines et retrahuntur a peccatis. Sed hec sunt ualde difficilia homini ad cognoscendum; unde de gloria dicitur Prou. "Que in celo sunt quis inuestigabit?" Et hoc quidem difficile est terrenis, quia "Qui de terra est, de terra loquitur": sed non est graue spiritualibus, quia "Qui de celo est" etc. Et ideo Dominus descendit de celo et incarnatus est, ut doceret nos celestia.

Erat etiam difficile cognoscere penas inferni: Sap. "Non est qui agnitus sit" etc.; et hoc dicitur in persona impiorum. Sed hoc non potest modo dici, quia sicut Christus descendit de celis ut doceret nos celestia, ita surrexit a mortuis ut doceret nos de inferis. Et ideo necesse est ut credamus quod non solum homo factus est et mortuus, sed quod etiam resurrexit a mortuis; et ideo dicitur 'Tertia die resurrexit a mortuis'.

Inuenimus autem quod multi resurrexerunt a mortuis, sicut Lazarus, filius uidue, filia archisynagogi; sed resurrectio Christi differt a resurrectione illorum et aliorum in quatuor.

Primo quantum ad causam resurrectionis; quia alii qui resurrexerunt, non resurrexerunt uirtute sua, sed uel Christi uel ad preces alicuius sancti. Sed Christus resurrexit uirtute propria, quia non solum erat homo sed Deus; et diuinitas numquam fuit separata nec ab anima nec a corpore. Et ideo corpus cum uoluit resumpsit animam, et anima corpus. Io. "Potestatem habeo ponendi animam" etc. Et licet

— VIII —

On the third day he rose from the dead.

Humanity must come to know two things, namely the glory of God and the pains of hell. Enticed through glory and frightened through pain, humankind becomes careful and draws back from sin. These things, however, remain extremely difficult to come to know. Thus Proverbs says about the glory [of God]: "[And with difficulty we search out the things that are on earth, and what is in sight we discover with effort.] Who will investigate the things that are in heaven?" (Prov. [Wis. 9:16]). And such investigation is indeed difficult for the earthly minded, because "The one who is of the earth, [belongs to the earth,] and speaks of the earth" [John 3:31]. But such investigation is not heavy for the spiritually minded, because "The one that comes from heaven [is above all things]" and so forth [John 3:31]. The Lord therefore descended from heaven and was enfleshed that he might teach us about heavenly things.

It remains also difficult to know the pains of hell: "There is no one known [to have come back from hell]" and so forth (Wis. [2:1]). And this is spoken in the voice of the wicked. But this no longer can be said, because just as Christ descended from heaven to teach us about heaven, so he rose from the dead to teach us about hell. Therefore we must believe that a human being not only is born and dies, but also that he or she rises from the dead. Thus it is said [in the creed]: "On the third day he rose from the dead."

We find, however, that many people rose from the dead, such as Lazarus, the son of the widow, and the daughter of the synagogue ruler. The resurrection of Christ differs from the resurrection of those and others in four ways.

(1) The cause of the resurrection differs. Others who rose [from the dead], did not rise by their own strength, but either by Christ's or by the prayers of some saint. But Christ rose by his own strength, because he was not only human but also God. His divinity was never separated from either his soul or his body. And therefore his body, when he wished, took up again his soul, and his soul, [when he wished,] took up again his body: ["No one takes my life from me, but

89

fuerit mortuus, hoc non fuit ex infirmitate nec necessitate, sed uirtute, quia sponte. Et hoc patet, quia, 'cum emisit spiritum, clamauit uoce magna': quod alii morientes facere non possunt, quia moriuntur ex infirmitate. Vnde et centurio dixit "Vere filius Dei erat iste".

Et ideo sicut sua uirtute posuit animam suam, ita uirtute sua suscepit; et ideo dicitur quod 'resurrexit', non quod fuerit resuscitatus ab alio: Ps. "Ego dormiui et resurrexi". Non est contrarium ei quod dixit Apostolus Ro. viii "Qui resuscitauit Ihesum a mortuis"; nam et Pater resuscitat eum, et Filius resurgit, quia eadem est uirtus Patris et Filii.

Secundo differt quantum ad uitam ad quam resurrexerunt, quia Christus ad uitam gloriosam et incorruptibilem, Ro. vi "Christus resurgens ex mortuis" etc.; alii ad eandem uitam quam prius habuerunt, sicut patet de Lazaro et aliis.

Tertio quantum ad uirtutem: quia uirtute resurrectionis Christi omnes resurgunt. Vnde Matth. "Multa corpora sanctorum" etc.; "Christus resurgens ex mortuis, primitie dormientium; quoniam quidem per hominem mors" etc. Sed uide quod Christus per passionem peruenit ad gloriam, Luce "Nonne sic oportuit Christum pati" etc., ut discas qualiter nos peruenire possimus: Act. "Per multas tribulationes" etc.

Quarto differt quantum ad tempus: quia resurrectio aliorum differtur usque ad finem mundi,[6] sed Christus resurrexit tertia die. Cuius ratio est quia natiuitas et mors et resurrectio Christi fuit propter salutem nostram; et ideo tunc uoluit resurgere quo salus nostra efficeretur. Vnde si statim resurrexisset, non fuisset creditum quod fuerit mortuus; item si multum distulisset, discipuli non remansissent in fide: et sic nulla utilitas fuisset in passione sua. Ps. "Que utilitas in

I lay it down by myself,] and I have the power to lay down my life, [and the power to take it up again]" and so forth (John [10:18]). Although Christ was dead, the reason was not exhaustion nor constraint, but rather strength, because [he died] by choice. This is clear, because "when he sent forth his spirit, he cried out with a loud voice" [Mt. 27:50]. Those others [the two thieves on either side] who were dying were not able to do so, because they died from exhaustion. Thus the centurion said: "Truly this man was the Son of God" [Mt. 27:54].

Just as Christ lay down his life by his own strength, so he took it up again by his own strength. Therefore it is said that "he rose," and not that he was resuscitated by another: "I slept [and I was over-come;] and I rose up, [because the Lord bore me up]" (Ps. [3:6]). Nor is this opposed to what Paul said in Romans 8: "God raised up this man Jesus, [of which we are all witnesses]" [Acts 2:32].[38] Indeed it is the Father who raised him up, and the Son who rose, because the Father and the Son share the same power.

(2) The life to which Christ rose differs, because Christ rose to a glorious and imperishable life: "As Christ rose from the dead [in the glory of the Father, so too we will walk in newness of life]" and so forth (Rom. 6:[4]). The others [who rose from the dead] came back to the same life as before, as is evident in the example of Lazarus and the rest.

(3) The power differs, because all rise up by virtue of the resurrection of Christ. Thus Matthew writes: ["And many tombs broke open,] and many of the bodies of the saints [who died rose up]" and so forth [27:52]. And "Christ rose from the dead, the first of those who have fallen asleep, because through a human being death [and through a human being resurrection from the dead]" and so forth [1 Cor. 15: 20–21]. Yet, do see that Christ came into his glory through the passion: "Was it not necessary that the Christ should suffer [and so enter into his glory?]" and so forth (Luke [24:26]), so that you might learn how we can enter into glory. "Through many tribulations [must we enter the kingdom of God]" and so forth (Acts [14:21]).

(4) The timing differs. The resurrection of all others is postponed until the end of the world, whereas Christ rose on the third day. The reason is that the birth, death, and resurrection of Christ was for our salvation. Therefore he wished to rise then so that our salvation might be brought about. If Christ had arisen immediately, there would be no credibility in his being dead. Similarly, if he much postponed his resurrection, the disciples would not have kept faith in him and no practical benefit would come from his passion: "What benefit from shedding my blood, [as long as I go down to corruption]" and so forth

sanguine meo?" etc. Et ideo tertia die resurrexit, ut crederetur mortuus, et ut discipuli non perderent fidem.

Possumus autem ex hiis quatuor ad eruditionem nostram accipere. Primo ut studeamus resurgere spiritualiter, a morte anime quam incurrit homo per peccatum, ad uitam iustitie que habetur per penitentiam : Apostolus "Exurge qui dormis" etc. ; et hec est resurrectio prima, Apoc. "Beatus qui habet partem" etc.

Item, non differamus resurgere usque ad mortem, sed cito, quia Christus tertia die resurrexit. Eccli. v "Ne tardes conuerti ad Dominum". Vel quia non poteris excogitare de resurrectione, infirmitate grauatus; et etiam perdis partem omnium bonorum que fiunt in Ecclesia.[7]

Item, ut resurgamus ad uitam incorruptibilem, scilicet quod non iterum moriamur; et in tali proposito quod non peccemus. Ro. "Christus resurgens ex mortuis iam non" etc.; "ita et nos existimate mortuos quidem peccato, uiuentes" etc.

Quarto, ut resurgamus ad uitam nouam et gloriosam, scilicet ut uitemus omnia que prius fuerunt occasiones et causa mortis et peccati. Ro. vi "Quomodo Christus resurrexit a mortuis per gloriam Patris, ita et nos in nouitate uite" etc. Et hec noua uita est uita iustitie, que innouat animam et perducit ad uitam glorie.

Ad quam etc.

(Ps. [29:10]). Thus he rose on the third day, that we might believe he was dead and that his disciples might not lose faith.

From these considerations above we can harvest four insights for our own learning. (1) We might study how to rise up spiritually from the death of the soul that a human being suffers through sin and rise to the life of justice that is obtained through penitence. Paul says: "Rise, you who sleep; [rise up from the dead, and Christ will enlighten you]" and so forth [Eph. 5:14]. This is the first resurrection: "Blessed [and holy] is the one who has part [in the first resurrection]" and so forth (Apoc. [20:6]).

(2) We might not postpone this rising until death, but [do it] quickly, because Christ rose on the third day: "Do not delay to be converted to the Lord [and do not put it off from day to day]" (Ecclus. [5:8]). [Do so now] because weighed down by infirmity you will not be able to think on the resurrection, or you also will lose part of all the good [merits and graces] that comes about in the church.[39]

(3) We might rise to an incorruptible life, that is to say, that we might not die again. With such a premise we might not sin. "Knowing that Christ risen from the dead no longer [dies; death no further overwhelms him]" and so forth (Rom. [6:9]). And "similarly you also should consider yourselves to be dead to sin, but alive [to God, in Christ Jesus, our Lord]" and so forth (Rom. [6:11]).

(4) We might rise to a new and glorious life, that is to say, that we might avoid what were previously occasion and cause of sin and death: "Just as Christ rose from the dead by the glory of the Father, so also [will we walk] in newness of life" and so forth (Rom. 6:[4]). This new life is a life of justice, which renews the soul and leads it on to the life of glory.

For which, [let us pray to the Lord] and so forth.

IX

This division of the Aquinas commentary concerns the meaning of the ascension. The reader will find an excellent example here of theology as faith seeking understanding, or reason in the service of revelation. Aquinas asks in what ways the ascension might be intelligible to reason. He answers: (1) Jesus should return home to his Father to complete his original mission; (2) Jesus' victory over the devil demands a victory enthronement; and (3) the humble in this life should justly be exalted.

There is little mention of the Session, when Jesus is enthroned to sit at the right hand of the Father. Just as Aquinas did not comment on the metaphor "father," in the title, "God, the Father-almighty," so here he does not comment upon the metaphorical situation of Jesus enthroned in glory and power at the right hand of God, the Father-almighty.

Ascendit ad celos, sedet ad dexteram Dei Patris omnipotentis.

Post Christi resurrectionem debemus credere ascensionem, quia Christus quadragesimo die ascendit; et ideo dicit 'Ascendit ad celos' etc. Circa quod tria nota: primo quod fuit sublimis, rationabilis et utilis.

Sublimis quidem, quia ascendit ad celos. Et hoc tripliciter exponitur. Primo, super omnes celos corporeos: Apostolus "Ascendit super omnes celos ut adimpleret omnia"; et hoc primo incepit in Christo, nam corpus terrenum non erat nisi in terra, in tantum etiam quod Adam fuerit in paradyso terrestri. Secundo, super omnes naturas spirituales constituit eum "in celestibus", et tamen "omnia subiecit" etc. Tertio, usque ad sedem Dei Patris: Dan. "Ecce in nubibus celi" etc., Marci ultimo "Dominus quidem Ihesus postquam" etc.

Non autem accepit in Deo dexteram corporaliter, sed methaphorice: quia in quantum Deus, dicitur sedere ad dexteram Dei Patris; in quantum homo, id est in potioribus bonis Patris. Et hoc affectauit dyabolus: Ysa. "Ascendam in montem testamenti" etc.; sed non peruenit nisi Christus, et ideo dicit 'Sedet ad dexteram Dei Patris'.

Secundo, hec ascensio fuit rationabilis quia ad celos; et hoc propter tria. Primo, quia celum debebatur Christo ex sua natura, naturale enim est ut unumquoque reuertatur unde trahit originem; principium originis Christi est a Deo qui est super omnia, et ideo dignum est ut ascenderet super omnia: Io. "Exiui a Patre" etc.; Io. "Nemo ascen-

He ascended into heaven, and sits at the right hand of God the Father almighty.

Following on the resurrection of Christ, we ought to believe in the ascension, because Christ ascended on the fortieth day [after the resurrection]. Therefore [in the creed] we read: "He ascended into heaven." Three points are noteworthy: in the first place, the ascension was (1) sublime, (2) intelligible, and (3) beneficial.

(1) The ascension was sublime because Christ ascended into heaven. There is a threefold explanation. (1.1) Above all the material heavens: "[He who descended, he it is who] ascends above all the heavens that he might fulfill all things." (Paul [Eph. 4:10]). This [ascension] first occurs in Christ, for an earthly body belongs only on the earth, and even Adam belonged in a terrestrial paradise. (1.2) Above all spiritual natures he established him "[raising him from the dead and seating him at his right hand] in heaven"; nonetheless, "all things are put [under his feet]" and so forth [Eph. 1:20–22]. (1.3) Even to the throne of God the Father: "And behold in the clouds of heaven [came one just like the Son of man]" and so forth (Dan. [7:13]). And in the last chapter of Mark, "The Lord Jesus after [he spoke to them was taken up into heaven and sits at the right hand of God]" and so forth [16:19].

The right hand of God must not be taken materially, but metaphorically. Considered as God, he [Christ] is said to sit at the right hand of the Father; considered as a human being he is said to sit with the high position of the Father. The devil pretended this: "[I will ascend above the heights of the mountains, and I will be like the Most High]" and so forth (Is. [14:13–14]).[40] No one, however, came so far but Christ, and therefore we read [in the creed]: "He sits at the right hand of God the Father."

(2) This ascension was intelligible because [it states] "into heaven." Three arguments pertain. (2.1) Heaven was owed to Christ by his very nature, for it is natural that each and every one of us return to where we take our origin. The starting principle of Christ stems from God who is above all things, and therefore it is fitting that Christ would ascend above all things: "I came forth from the Father, [and

dit nisi qui de celo descendit" etc. Et licet sancti ascenderint in celum et ascendant, non tamen sicut Christus; quia Christus sua uirtute, sancti autem tracti a Christo: Cant. "Trahe me post te" etc. Vel potest dici quia nemo ascendit in celum nisi Christus, quia sancti non ascendunt nisi in quantum sunt membra Christi, qui est caput Ecclesie.

Item, ex sua uictoria. Nam Christus missus est in mundum contra dyabolum et uicit eum, et ideo meruit exaltari super omnia: Apoc. "Qui uicerit, faciam illum sedere in throno meo" etc.

Item ex sua humilitate. Nulla autem humilitas fuit ita magna sicut humilitas Christi, qui cum esset Deus uoluit homo fieri, cum esset Dominus accepit formam serui et factus est obediens usque ad mortem, et etiam descendit ad infernum: et ideo meruit exaltari usque ad sedem Dei, nam humilitas est uia ad exaltationem: Matth. "Qui se humiliat, exaltabitur"; Eph. "Qui descendit, ipse est et qui ascendit".

Fuit etiam hec ascensio utilis quantum ad tria. Primo quantum ad conductum: nam ad hoc ascendit ut nos duceret; sicut enim resurrexit ut nos resurgere faceret, ita ascendit ut nos duceret; nos enim nesciebamus uiam, sed ipse fecit: Mich. "Ascendit, pandens iter" etc. Similiter etiam ad hoc ascendit ut assecuraret nos de possessione regni celestis: Io. "Vado parare uobis locum".

Secundo, quantum ad securitatem: ad hoc enim ascendit ut interpellaret pro nobis. Apostolus "Ascendens per semet ipsum ad Deum ut interpellaret" etc.; Io. "Hec scribo uobis ut non peccetis" etc., "propitiatio" etc.

I came into the world; again I leave the world, and I go to the Father]" and so forth (John [16:28]). And "No one ascends [into heaven] except the one who descends from heaven, [the Son of man, who is in heaven]" and so forth (John [3:13]). And although the saints have ascended and will ascend, nonetheless they do not ascend like Christ. He ascended by his own power, but the saints are drawn by Christ: "Draw me on, [we will run in the scent of your perfume] after you" and so forth [Song [1:3]). Or one could argue no one ascends into heaven but Christ, because the saints do not ascend except as members of Christ, who is the head of the church.

(2.2.) [Intelligible] from his own victory. Christ was sent into the world against the devil and he conquered him, and therefore he merits to be exalted above all things: "The one who conquers I will make to sit on my throne [with me, just as I conquered and I was seated with my Father on his throne]" and so forth (Apoc. [3:21]).

(2.3) [Intelligible] from his humility. No humility was as great as the humility of Christ, who when he was God wished to become human, who when he was Lord took the form of a servant and was made obedient even unto death; he also descended into hell. Therefore he merited to be exalted even to the throne of God, for humility is the way to exaltation: "Whoever humbles himself will be exalted" (Mt. [Luke 14:11]). And "The one who came down, he is the one who goes up [above all the heavens, in order to fulfill all things]" (Eph. [4:10]).

(3) This ascension [of Christ] was beneficial for three reasons. (3.1) With regard to conduct. Christ ascended so that he might lead us. Just as he rose that he might enable us to rise, so he ascends that he might lead us. Indeed we do not know the way, but he made it: "Laying open the way he ascends [before them . . . and the Lord at their head]" and so forth (Mic. [2:13]). In like manner, he ascended that he might secure for us possession of the heavenly kingdom: "[In my Father's house there are many mansions]. . . . I go to prepare a place for you" (John [14:2]).

(3.2) With regard to secureness. Christ ascended so that he might intercede for us. Paul writes: "[Thus he can save forever those who] draw near to God through him, living always to intercede for us" and so forth [Heb. 7:25].[41] And "[My children,] I am writing this to you so that you might not sin," and so forth "[but if anyone does sin, we have an advocate with the Father, Jesus Christ the just one. And he is a] propitiation [for our sins, and not only for our own, but also for the whole world's]" and so forth (1 John [2:1–2]).

Tertio, ut traheret ad se corda nostra: Matth. "Vbi est oculus tuus" etc. Ex hoc contemnimus temporalia, Col. "Si consurrexistis cum Christo" etc.

(3.3) That Christ might draw our hearts to himself: "Where your eye is, [there also is your heart]" and so forth (Mt. [6:21]).[42] Consequently, we will spurn earthly things: "If you have risen up together with Christ, [seek the things that are above, where Christ is seated at the right hand of God]" and so forth (Col. [3:1]).

X

This division of the Aquinas commentary concerns the meaning of the judgment to come of the living and the dead. More than with any other section, the contemporary reader will have difficulty understanding Aquinas here. He would make Christ into a stern judge, before whom one should be sore afraid. Egocentric motivation that seems self-serving is disturbing. Thus avoidance of hell from fear, or attainment of heaven from reward seem meretricious to us. And yet, one wonders if human beings ever outgrow the need for such motivation, partly from fear of negative consequences and partly from hope of positive emoluments. The constant warnings about nuclear holocaust and the nuclear night that are preached by contemporary scientist and politician alike remind this observer of the old-fashioned hellfire sermons of Christianity of yesteryear.

Moreover, it must be remembered that these remarks were given by Aquinas in church sermons delivered in Lent during the Middle Ages. The people expected to hear of an awesome and terrible judgment and would probably have been disappointed not to hear such a theology. That is not to defend this theology as being without short-comings and distortions, as have all theologies.

Perhaps an even greater problem is the insistence upon the individual judgment or particular judgment at the expense of equal consideration of the general judgment, when all the world will be justified before God and before humankind. We are saved in the community that is the church, and we are saved as a human race, for all of whom Christ died. A fear-and-reward judgment suffers not only from the quality of its motivation but also from the isolation of its focus upon the individual.

103

Inde uenturus est iudicare uiuos et mortuos.

Ad officium domini et regis spectat iudicare: Prou. "Rex qui sedet in solio iudicii" etc. Quia igitur Christus ascendit in celum, et sedet ad dexteram Dei ut dominus omnium, manifestum est quod ad eum spectat iudicium: et ideo in regula catholice fidei confitemur quod 'uenturus est iudicare uiuos et mortuos'. Hoc etiam angeli dixerunt discipulis: Act. i. "Quemadmodum uidistis eum" etc.

Sunt autem tria consideranda de hoc iudicio : primum est forma iudicii, secundum est quod iudicium istud sit timendum, tertium est qualiter preparemus nos ad hoc iudicium.

Primo, ad formam iudicii tria concurrunt: scilicet quis sit iudex, qui iudicandi, et de quibus. Iudex est Christus: Act. "Hic est qui constitutus est a Deo iudex" etc., siue accipiamus per uiuos recte uiuentes et per mortuos peccatores, siue per uiuos ad litteram illos qui tunc uiuentes, et per mortuos omnes qui mortui sunt.

Est autem iudex non solum in quantum Deus, sed etiam in quantum homo; et hoc propter tria. Primo quia necessarium est quod iudicati iudicem uideant; Deitas autem ita est delectabilis quod nullus potest eam uidere sine gaudio, et ideo nullus dampnandus poterit eam uidere, quia tunc gauderet. Et ideo necesse est quod appareat sub forma hominis, ut ab omnibus uideatur. Io. "Potestatem dedit ei iudicium facere quia filius" etc.

Secundo quia ipse meruit hoc officium secundum quod homo: ipse enim secundum quod homo fuit iniuste iudicatus, et ex hoc Deus

From where he will come to judge the living and the dead.

To oversee judication belongs to the office of the lord and king: "The king who sits on the throne of judgment [drives out all evil with his scrutiny]" and so forth (Prov. [20:8]). Therefore, because Christ ascended into heaven, and sits at the right hand of God as lord of all, to oversee judgment clearly belongs to him. Thus in the rule of catholic faith[43] we confess that "he will come again to judge the living and the dead." The angels indeed said as much to the disciples: "[Men of Galilee, why do you stand here gazing into heaven? This Jesus, who has been taken from you into heaven, will come again] in the same way as you have seen him [going into heaven]" and so forth (Acts 1:[11]).

Three points about this judgment are noteworthy: (1) the form of the judgment; (2) the judgment should be feared; and (3) how we shall prepare ourselves for this judgment.

(1) As to the form of the judgment, there are three strands: (1.1) who is judge, (1.2) who are the judged, and (1.3) what about them. (1.1) The judge is Christ: "[And he began to preach to the people and to testify that] he is the one who is established by God as judge [of the living and the dead]" and so forth (Acts [10:42]). This obtains whether we interpret the *living* to be those who are living virtuously and the *dead* to be sinners, or we interpret the *living* to be literally those then alive and the *dead* to be all those who ever died.

Christ is judge not only as God but also as a human being. There are three reasons. (1.11) Those being judged must see the judge. The Godhead, however, is so delightful that nobody can see it without joy, and thus anybody damned would not be able to see it, for then they would rejoice. Therefore [the judge] must appear in the form of a human being, so that he might be seen by everyone: "And he [the Father] gave to him [the Son] power to render judgment, because he is the Son [of man]" and so forth (John [5:27]).

(1.12) Christ merited this office [of judge] precisely because he was human. Insofar as he was a human being, Christ was unjustly judged. For this reason God made him judge of the whole world: "Your

105

fecit eum iudicem totius mundi. Iob "Causa tua quasi impii iudicata est".

Tertio ut cesset desperatio ab hominibus, si ab homine iudicantur: si enim solus Deus iudicaret, homines territi desperarent. Matth. "Videbunt Filium hominis" etc.

Iudicandi uero sunt omnes homines qui sunt et qui fuerunt et erunt: Cor. "Omnes nos astare oportet" etc. Est autem, sicut Gregorius dicit, differentia inter iudicandos: quia iudicandi aut sunt boni, aut sunt mali. Malorum autem quidam dampnabuntur et non iudicabuntur, scilicet infideles, quorum facta non discutientur, quia "qui non credit iam iudicatus est", Io. Quidam uero condempnabuntur et iudicabuntur, scilicet fideles decedentes in mortali peccato: Ro. "Stipendia peccati mors est"; non enim excludentur a iudicio propter fidem quam habuerunt.

Bonorum etiam quidam saluabuntur et non iudicabuntur, scilicet pauperes spiritu propter Deum; immo iudicabunt alios: Matth. "Vos qui secuti estis me" etc. Et hoc intelligitur non solum de duodecim apostolis, sed etiam de omnibus pauperibus; alias Paulus non esset de eis, et tamen dicit "An nescitis quoniam angelos iudicabimus?" Ysa. "Dominus ad iudicium ueniet" etc.

Quidam saluabuntur et iudicabuntur, scilicet decedentes in iustitia. Licet enim in iustitia decesserint, tamen propter occupationem temporalium in aliquo lapsi sunt; et ideo iudicabuntur, sed saluabuntur. Iudicabuntur autem de omnibus factis, bonis et malis: Eccl. "Ambula in uiis cordis tui" etc., "iudicium" etc. Item etiam de uerbis otio-

cause was judged as if one of the wicked, [you will receive vindication and judgment]" (Job [36:17]).

(1.13) If men and women are judged by a human being, their desperation might be curtailed: "[And then] they will see the Son of man [coming on a cloud with great power and majesty!" and so forth (Mt. [Luke 21:27]).

(1.2) The judged are all men and women who are, who were, and who will be: "All of us must stand [before the tribunal of Christ, that each one might retrieve their own deeds done in the body, whether for good or for bad]" and so forth (2 Cor. [5:10]). As Gregory says,[44] there is a [fourfold] distinction among those judged.

(1.3) Those being judged are either good or they are bad.

(1.31) Of the bad people, however, some are indeed damned and not judged, that is to say, the unbelievers, whose deeds are not debated, because ["Whoever believes in him will not be judged,] and whoever does not believe is already judged" (John [3:18]).

(1.32) There are others, however, who will be condemned and be judged, that is to say, the believers who have fallen into mortal sin: "The wages of sin is death" (Rom. [6:23]). They will not be excluded from judgment [and condemnation] on account of their faith.

(1.33) Of the good people, there are some who will be saved and will not be judged, that is to say, the poor in spirit for God's sake. Moreover, they will judge others: "[Amen I say to you,] you who followed me [in the redressing, when the Son of man will sit on his throne in his majesty, you all will sit on twelve thrones, judging the twelve tribes of Israel]" (Mt. [19:28]). This is to be understood not only of the twelve apostles, but also of all the poor [in spirit]. Otherwise Paul would not be one of them, and nevertheless he says: "Do you not know you will judge the angels?" [1 Cor. 6:3]. And "The Lord will come into judgment [with the elders of the people and its leaders]" and so forth (Is. [3:14]).

(1.34) There are also others [among the good people] who will be saved and be judged, that is to say those who have died in [a state of] justice. Although they have died in justice, nonetheless they have fallen because of being occupied with temporal affairs in some way. Therefore they will be judged, yet saved. They will be judged, however, on all their deeds, good and bad: "[Rejoice young people in your youth, and may your heart be good to you all the days of your young life.] Walk in the ways of your heart [and in the vision of your eyes, and know that for all this God will bring you into judgment]" and so forth (Eccles. [11:9]). And "[All things God will bring to] judgment [for any mistake, either for good or for bad]" and so forth (Eccles. [12:14]).

sis: Matth. "Omne uerbum otiosum" etc.; item de cogitationibus, quia "in cogitationibus hominis interrogatio erit".

Sic ergo patet de forma iudicii.

Est autem iudicium istud timendum propter quatuor. Primum est sapientia iudicis. Prou. "Omnes uie hominis" etc. Ipse enim scit uerba nostra, Prou. "Auris zeli" etc.; item cogitationes nostras, Ier. "Prauum est cor hominis et inscrutabile" etc. Ibi erunt testes infallibiles, scilicet consciencie hominum: Sap. "Cogitationibus" etc.; "inuicem" etc.

Secundum est potentia iudicis, quia omnipotens in se: Ysa. "Ecce Dominus in fortitudine ueniet" etc. Item omnipotens in aliis, quia tunc omnis creatura cum eo erit: Sap. "Pugnabit pro eo orbis terrarum" etc.; et ideo dicebat Iob "Non est qui de manu tua possit eruere".

Tertium est iustitia inflexibilis. Nunc enim est tempus misericordie, sed tunc solum iustitie; nunc est tempus nostrum, sed tunc erit tempus Dei: Ps. "Cum accepero tempus" etc.: Prou. "Zelus et furor uiri" etc.

Quartum est ira iudicis. Aliter enim apparebit iustis, quia dulcis, delectabilis et benignus: Ysa. "Regem in decore suo uidebunt"; sed malis apparebit iratus et timendus: Ysa. "Dicent montibus: cadite" etc. Ira enim hec in Deo non dicit commotionem animi sed effectum ire, scilicet penam inflictam peccatoribus.[8]

Debemus enim quatuor remedia habere contra hunc timorem. Primum est bona opera: Apost. "Vis non timere potestatem?" etc. Iob "Fugite a facie gladii, quoniam ultor iniquitatis" etc. Secundum est confessio et penitentia de commissis; in qua tria debent esse: dolor

Similarly, with idle words: "[I say to you, for] every idle word, [that humankind shall have spoken, they will give an account for it, on the day of judgment]" and so forth (Mt. [12:36]). Likewise with thoughts, because "there will be questioning into the thoughts of humankind" [Wis. 1:9].[45]

The "form of judgment" is thus evident.

(2) This judgment should be feared for four reasons. (2.1) The wisdom of the judge: "All the ways of humankind [lie open to his eyes, a discerner of spirits is the Lord]" and so forth [Prov. [16:2]). He knows our words: "A jealous ear [hears everything and the whisper of murmurings is not concealed]" and so forth (Prov. [Wis. 1:10]). He knows our thoughts: "Corrupt is the heart of everyone and inscrutable, [who knows it?]" and so forth (Jer. [17:9]). Infallible witnesses will be there [in the judgment], that is to say, the consciences of humanity: "[Which shows the law written in their hearts, and their conscience bears witness, while their] thoughts" and so forth "conflict, [accusing or even excusing]" and so forth (Wis. [Rom. 2:15]).

(2.2) The power of the judge, who is of himself all-powerful: "Behold the Lord God will come in strength, [and his right arm will conquer]" and so forth (Is. [40:10]). Similarly, he is all-powerful with others, because every creature will then be in his presence: "The whole world will fight for him [against the unwise]" and so forth (Wis. [5:21]). Therefore we read: "[Though you know I do nothing wicked,] no one can be delivered from your hand" (Job [10:7]).

(2.3) Unbending justice. Now is the time for mercy, but then for only justice. Now is our time, but then will be God's time: "At the appointed time, [I will judge with justice]" and so forth (Ps. 74:3]). And "Jealousy and fury in a man does not spare on the day of revenge" and so forth (Prov. [6:34]).

(2.4) The anger of the judge. He [the judge] will appear otherwise to the just, because he is mild, agreeable and kind: "His eyes will see the king in his beauty, [they will behold the land to its extent]" (Is. [33:17]). However, he will appear wrathful and fearful to the unjust: "They will say to the mountains: fall upon [us, and hide us from the face of him who is seated on the throne]" and so forth (Is. [Apoc. 6:16]). This anger in God does not mean a commotion of soul, but the effect of anger, that is to say, the punishment inflicted upon sinners.

(3) We ought to have four antidotes against this fear [of judgment]. (3.1) Good works: "Do you wish not to fear authority? [Do good, and you will have praise from it]" and so forth (Rom. [13:3]). And "Flee from the face of the sword, because the avenger of iniquity [is a sword]" and so forth (Job [19:29]). (3.2) Confession and penance for sins com-

in contritione, pudor in confessione et acerbitas in satisfactione, que expiant penam eternam. Tèrtium est eleemosyna: Matth. "Facite uo-bis amicos" etc. Quartum est caritas, quia "uniuersa delicta operit"⁹ etc.

mitted, about which there ought to be three things: sorrow in contrition, shame in confession, and stringency in the satisfaction, which expiates eternal punishment. (3.3) Giving alms: "Make for yourselves friends [of the Mammon of iniquity, so that when you fail, they will receive you into eternal dwelling places]" and so forth (Mt. [Luke 16:9]). (3.4) Charity [love], because "[charity] makes up for a multitude of sins" and so forth [1 Pet. 4:8].[46]

XI

This division of the Aquinas commentary concerns the meaning of the Holy Spirit as the love of God that fills the soul and is the promised gift that the risen Jesus sends to his church. Aquinas outlines the Niceno-Constantinopolitan interpolations written in the Council of Constantinople (381), which defend the Holy Spirit as truly God equally adored with the Father and with the Son. His treatment is classical and inspirational. Aquinas does not enter into the "filioque" controversy, as he does in his conciliatory opusculum, "Contra Errores Graecorum."

Just as knowledge leads to love, so faith leads to the Holy Spirit. The spirit re-creates, and thus the repair of a fallen world falls to the Spirit. Indwelling in the Christian, the Spirit illumines the mind and enkindles the heart, just as fire gives both light and warmth.

Credo in Spiritum Sanctum.

Sicut dictum est, Verbum Dei est Filius Dei sicut uerbum hominis dicitur conceptus intellectus. Sed quandoque homo habet uerbum mortuum, quando scilicet cogitat que facere debet, sed tamen uoluntas faciendi non adest ei; sicut quando homo credit et non operatur, fides eius dicitur mortua. Verbum autem Dei est uiuum: Hebr. "Viuus est sermo Dei et efficax", et ideo necesse est quod Deus habeat bonam uoluntatem secum et amorem: Augustinus in libro De Trinitate "Verbum quod insinuare intendimus cum amore notitia est".

Sicut autem Verbum Filius Dei est, ita amor Dei est Spiritus Sanctus; et inde est quod tunc homo habet Spiritum Sanctum quando diligit Deum: Apostolus "Caritas Dei diffusa est" etc. Sicut autem Spiritus Dei nichil est aliud nisi amor quo Deus se diligit et nos, ita in nobis Spiritus Sanctus est quando diligimus Deum et proximum.

Fuerunt autem aliqui qui male sentientes de Spiritu Sancto, dixerunt quod erat creatura, et quod minor Patre et Filio, et erat minister Dei. Et ideo sancti patres ad remouendum hunc errorem addiderunt quinque uerba in alio Symbolo de Spiritu Sancto.

Primum est quod licet sint alii spiritus, scilicet angeli, sunt tamen ministri Dei secundum illud Apostoli "Omnes sunt administratorii spiritus" etc.; sed Spiritus Sanctus est Dominus, et inde est quod "ubi est Spiritus Domini, ibi est libertas"; cuius ratio est quia aufert timorem mundi et facit diligere Deum: Cor. "Dominus est Spiri-

—XI—

I believe in the Holy Spirit.

Just as the word of a human being is said to be the concept of the intellect, so the Word of God is the Son of God. But, whenever anyone has a dead word, then they think about what they ought to do, yet the will to do it is not present in them. Similarly, when anyone believes but does not practice, their faith is said to be dead. The word of God, however, is alive: "The word of God is living and potent, [more penetrating than any double-edged sword, probing even to the separation of soul and spirit, of joints and marrow, a discerner of the thoughts and intentions of the heart]" (Heb. [4:12]). Therefore it must be that God possesses goodwill and love from within. Augustine writes in "De Trinitate":[47] "The word that we are trying to suggest is an intimate knowing together with love."

Just as the Word [of God] is the Son of God, so the love of God is the Holy Spirit. Thus it is that a man or woman has the Holy Spirit when he or she loves God. Paul writes: "[But hope is not undone, because] the love of God is poured out [in our hearts through the Holy Spirit, who is given to us]" and so forth [Rom. 5:5]. And just as the Spirit of God is nothing other than the love in which God loves himself and us, so the Holy Spirit dwells in us when we love God and neighbor.

There were some [persons], however, who expressed bad thinking about the Holy Spirit. They said the Spirit was a creature, was less than the Father and the Son, and was a minister of God. Therefore, to remove this error, the holy fathers [of the Council of Constantinople] added five phrases about the Holy Spirit in the other symbol [the Niceno-Constantinopolitan Creed].

(1) Although other spirits may exist, that is to say, angels, who are but ministers of God according to Paul: "Are they not all ministering spirits [sent in service on account of those who will take hold of the inheritance of salvation]" and so forth [Heb. 1:14]. Nevertheless, the Holy Spirit is Lord. Thus it remains that "where the Spirit of the Lord is, there is freedom" [2 Cor. 3:17]. The reason is that the Holy Spirit takes away fear of the world and enables [us] to love God:

tus" etc. Et ideo dicitur 'Credo in Spiritum Sanctum Dominum'.

Secundum est quia in hoc est uita anime que coniungit Deo, cum Deus sit uita anime; Deo autem coniungit Spiritus Sanctus per amorem quia ipse est amor Dei, et ideo uiuificat: Io. "Spiritus est qui uiuificat" etc. Et ideo dicitur 'et uiuificantem'.

Tertium est quod Spiritus Sanctus est eiusdem substantie cum Patre et Filio, quia sicut Filius est Verbum Patris, ita Spiritus Sanctus est amor Patris et Filii, et ideo procedit ab utroque; et sicut Verbum Dei est eiusdem substantie cum Patre, ita et amor cum Patre et Filio: et ideo dicitur 'Qui ex Patre Filioque procedit'. Vnde et per hoc patet quod non est creatura.

Quartum est quod est equalis Patri et Filio quantum ad cultum: Eph. "Nos autem qui sumus uera circumcisio" etc. Et ideo dicitur 'Qui cum Patre et Filio simul adoratur'.

Quintum, per quod manifestatur quod est equalis Deo, quia prophete locuti sunt ab eo. Constat autem quod, si Spiritus Sanctus non esset Deus, non diceretur quod prophete locuti sunt ab eo; sed Petrus dicit quod sic "Spiritu Sancto inspirati" etc.; Ysa. "Et nunc misit me Dominus et Spiritus eius". Et ideo dicitur 'Qui locutus est per prophetas'.

Per hoc autem destruuntur duo errores; scilicet Manicheorum, qui dixerunt quod Vetus testamentum non erat a bono Deo; sed falsum est, quia Spiritus Sanctus locutus est per prophetas. Item Priscille et Montani, qui dixerunt quod prophete non sunt locuti a Spiritu Sancto, sed quasi amentes.

Prouenit autem nobis multiplex fructus a Spiritu Sancto. Primo enim purgat a peccatis. Cuius ratio est quia eiusdem est reficere cuius est constituere; anima autem creatur per Spiritum Sanctum, quia om-

"The Lord is Spirit" and so forth [2 Cor. 3:17]. Thus we read [in the Niceno-Constantinopolitan Creed] "I believe in the Holy Spirit, Lord."

(2) The life of the soul lies in its union with God, inasmuch as God is the life of the soul. The Holy Spirit is united to God through love, because the Holy Spirit is the love of God, and therefore gives life: "It is the Spirit that gives life; [the flesh profits not at all]" and so forth (John [6:64]). Thus we read [in the Niceno-Constantinopolitan Creed] "and life-giver."

(3) The Holy Spirit is of the same substance with the Father and Son, because just as the Son is the Word of the Father, so the Holy Spirit is the love of the Father and Son, and thus proceeds from them both. Just as the Word of God is of the same substance with the Father, so the love [of God is of the same substance] with the Father and Son. And thus we read [in the Niceno-Constantinopolitan Creed] "Who proceeds from the Father and the Son." Therefore it is clear that the Holy Spirit is not a creature.

(4) The Holy Spirit is equal to the Father and the Son in regard to worship: "We are the true circumcision [who serve God in the spirit, and glory in Christ Jesus, and who do not put their trust in the flesh]" and so forth (Eph. [Phil. 3:3]). And thus we read [in the Niceno-Constantinopolitan Creed] "Who with the Father and Son is likewise adored."

(5) The Holy Spirit is shown to be equal to God because the prophets spoke in the Spirit. Thus if the Holy Spirit were not God, it would not be said that the prophets spoke in God. But Peter so says: "[For prophecy never came about by human will, but holy people,] inspired by the Holy Spirit, [spoke of God]" and so forth [2 Pet. 1:21]. And in Isaiah: "[Draw near to me and listen. From the beginning I have not spoken in secret; from the time before it came to be, I was there;] and now the Lord God and his Spirit sent me" [48:16]. Thus we read [in the Niceno-Constantinopolitan Creed] "Who spoke through the prophets."

By this two errors are overcome: that is to say, (1) the Manicheans who said that the Old Testament was not from a good God. But this is false, because the Holy Spirit spoke through the prophets. Similarly, (2) Priscilla and Montanus,[48] who said that the prophets did not speak in the Holy Spirit, but they were more or less out of their minds [entranced].

Manifold fruit befalls us from the Holy Spirit. (1) The Spirit cleanses from sins. The reason is that remaking belongs to the one who first made. The soul, however, is created through the Holy Spirit,

nia per ipsum facit Deus: Deus enim diligendo suam bonitatem creat omnia. Sap. "Diligis omnia" etc.; Dyonisius "Diuinus amor non permisit eum sine germine esse". Oportet ergo quod corda hominum per peccatum destructa reficiantur a Spiritu Sancto: Ps. "Emitte Spiritum tuum et creabunter" etc. Nec mirum si Spiritus Sanctus purgat, quia omnia peccata dimittuntur per amorem, Prou. "Vniuersa delicta operit caritas".

Secundo illuminat intellectum, quia omnia que scimus sunt a Spiritu Sancto: Io. "Paraclitus autem Spiritus Sanctus" etc.; idem "Vnctio docebit uos omnia".

Tertio agit ad seruandum mandata. Nullus autem posset seruare mandata Dei nisi amaret Deum: Io. "Si quis diligit me" etc.; amare autem Deum facit Spiritus Sanctus, Ysa. xxxvi "Aufert a uobis cor lapideum" etc.

Quarto confirmat spem eterne uite, quia est sicut pignus illius hereditatis: Apostolus "Signati estis Spiritu Sancto qui est pignus" etc.; est enim quasi arra uite eterne. Cuius ratio est quia ex hoc debetur uita eterna homini in quantum efficitur filius Dei; hoc autem fit per hoc quod efficitur similis Christo. Assimilantur autem aliqui Christo per hoc quod habent Spiritum Christi, qui est Spiritus Sanctus: Gal. "Non enim accepistis spiritum seruitutis" etc.; idem "Quoniam estis filii Dei, misit Deus" etc.

because God made everything through him.[49] Indeed, in loving his own goodness God created everything: "You love all things [that be, and nothing of what you have made do you hate]" and so forth (Wis. [11:25]). And [Pseudo-]Dionysius[50] writes: "Divine love did not permit him to be without issue." Therefore, the hearts of men destroyed by sin should be remade by the Holy Spirit: "Send forth your Spirit and they will be created; [and you will renew the face of the earth]" and so forth (Ps. [103:30]). No wonder the Holy Spirit cleanses [from sins], because all sins are taken away through love: "[Hatred excites strife, but] charity manages all offenses" [Prov. [10:12]].[51]

(2) The Holy Spirit enlightens the intellect, because everything we know comes by the Holy Spirit: "The Paraclete, the Holy Spirit, [whom the Father will send in my name, he will teach you everything, and prompt you in everything whatsoever that I shall have said to you]" and so forth (John [14:26]). And similarly: "[And you who have received anointing from him, may it abide in you; and you have no need that someone should teach you, since] his anointing will teach you all things." [1 John 2:27].

(3) The Holy Spirit brings us to keep the commandments. No one can keep the commandments of God unless he love God: "If anyone loves me, [they will keep my commandment, and then my Father will love them, and we will come to them, and make our dwelling with them]" and so forth (John [14:23]). However, the Holy Spirit enables us to love God: "[I will give you a new heart, and I will put a new spirit in your breast;] and I will take away the heart of stone [from your flesh, and I will give you a heart of flesh. And I will put my Spirit in your breast]" and so forth (Is. [Ezek. 36:26–27]).

(4) The Holy Spirit confirms [our] hope of eternal life, because the Spirit is like a token of that inheritance. Paul writes: "You have been sealed with the [promised] Holy Spirit, who is the pledge [of our inheritance, until we take possession, in the praise of his glory]" and so forth [Eph. 1:13–14]. Indeed, the Spirit is, as it were, the guarantor of eternal life. The reason is because eternal life is due to a human being insofar as he or she has been made a child of God. This comes about, however, through being made like to Christ. People are made like to Christ through having the Spirit of Christ, which is the Holy Spirit: "You have not received the spirit of servitude [again in fear, but rather you have received the spirit of adoption of children, in which we cry out: Abba, Father]" and so forth (Gal. [Rom. 8:15]). Similarly, "Because you are children of God, God sent [the Spirit of his Son into your hearts, crying out: Abba, Father]" and so forth [Gal. 4:6].

Quinto consulit in dubiis, et que sit uoluntas Dei: Apoc. "Qui habet aures" etc., "quid Spiritus" etc.; Ysa. "Ego quasi magistrum audiam eum" etc.

(5) The Holy Spirit counsels [us] in [our] doubts about what may be the will of God: "Who has ears, [let him hear] what the Spirit [says to the Churches: I will give to him who conquers to eat of the tree of life, which is in the paradise of my God]" and so forth (Apoc. [2:7]). And in Isaiah: "[In the morning he awakens, he awakens hearing in me,] that I might hear him as if taught" and so forth [50:4].

This division of the Aquinas commentary concerns the meaning of the holy catholic church. Aquinas follows the traditional four marks of the church mentioned in the Nicene Creed: (1) one church, without division, although not without multiplicity; (2) holy church, washed in the blood of Christ, anointed by the Holy Spirit, who dwells therein; (3) catholic church, universal in space even to the ends of the world, as well as in time, reaching back to the past of the souls departed and looking forward to the future of the "church triumphant"; and (4) the perduring church, founded on the rock that is Christ, and founded secondarily upon the twelve Apostles, with Peter as the rock of Christ.

Aquinas's treatment of the church presents the classical theology. His description of the fourth mark as "perduring" departs from the more customary word "apostolic." The meaning is, however, the same, although "apostolic" also captures the dimension of being sent to the ends of the world to preach the good news.

Sanctam Ecclesiam catholicam.

Sicut uidemus quod in uno homine est una anima et unum corpus, et tamen sunt diuersa membra ipsius, sic et Ecclesia catholica est unum corpus et habet diuersa membra. Quod autem hoc corpus uiuificat, est Spiritus Sanctus; et ideo post fidem de Spiritu Sancto, iubemur credere sanctam Ecclesiam catholicam. Et ideo dicitur in Symbolo 'Sanctam Ecclesiam catholicam'.

Circa quod sciendum est primo quod ecclesia idem est quod congregatio; unde Ecclesia sancta idem est quod congregatio fidelium, et quilibet homo christianus est sicut membrum huius Ecclesie, de qua dicitur Prou. "Appropiate ad me indocti" etc. Habet autem hec Ecclesia sancta quatuor conditiones: quia una, quia sancta, quia catholica, id est uniuersalis, et quia fortis.

Quantum ad primum sciendum est quod, licet diuersi heretici diuersas sectas adinuenerint, non tamen pertinent ad ecclesiam quia sunt diuisi in partes; sed Ecclesia est una: Cant. "Vna est columba mea". Causatur autem unitas Ecclesie ex tribus: primo ex unitate fidei. Omnes enim christiani idem credunt corde et confitentur ore, Cor. "Idipsum dicatis omnes et non sint in uobis scismata"; et inde est quod dicit ipse "Vnus Dominus et una fides".

Secundo ex unitate spei, quia omnes firmati sunt in spe perueniendi ad uitam eternam: Apostolus "Vnus spiritus, unum corpus, sicut uocauit nos" etc.

Tertio ex unitate caritatis, quia omnes connectuntur in amore

— XII —

The holy catholic church.

Just as we have seen [in natural philosophy, for example] that in one human being there is one soul and one body, and yet there are diverse members, so the catholic church is one body and yet has diverse members. What [as its soul] animates this body, however, is the Holy Spirit. And so, after faith in the Holy Spirit, we are told to believe in the holy catholic church. Thus we read in the symbol [the Apostles' Creed], "holy catholic church."

Concerning the church, we ought to know first of all that "church" is the same [in meaning] as "congregation." Thus the holy church is the same as the congregation of the faithful. Any Christian man or woman whatever is a member, as it were, of this church, about which Proverbs says: "Draw near to me, you untaught, [and gather yourselves into the house of learning]" and so forth (Prov. [Ecclus. 51:31]).[52] This holy church, however, has four characteristics [traditionally called "marks"]: that it is (1) one, (2) holy, (3) catholic (that is, universal), and (4) perduring.

(1) As to the first characteristic, we should know this. Although diverse heretics have founded diverse sects, they nevertheless do not belong to the church, because they are divided into parts, whereas the church is one: "One is my dove, [my perfect one, the only one of her mother, the chosen one of her who bore her]" (Song [6:8]). The unity of the church is caused by three virtues. (1.1) From the unity of faith. Indeed all Christians believe the same thing in their heart and confess it with their tongue: "[I appeal to you, brethren, through the name of Our Lord Jesus Christ,] that all of you may say the same thing, and that there be no split among you" (1 Cor. [1:10]). And thus it is that Paul says: "One Lord and one faith, [one baptism]" [Eph. 4:5].

(1.2) From the unity of hope. All Christians are confirmed in the hope of attaining eternal life. Paul writes: "One spirit, one body, as he called us [as you were called in the one hope of your vocation]" and so forth [Eph. 4:4].[53]

(1.3) From the unity of charity. In the love of God, all Christians are joined together with one another in a mutual love: I wish "that

Dei et ad inuicem in amore mutuo: Io. Volo "ut sint unum" etc. Manifestatur autem huiusmodi amor quando membra pro se inuicem sol-
licita sunt, et quando sibi inuicem compatiuntur: Eph. "Totum corpus connexum et compactum" etc , quia quodlibet de officio suo seu
aliqua gratia aliis debet seruire. Nota autem quod nullus debet con-
temnere abici ab ista Ecclesia, quia non est nisi una Ecclesia in qua
homines saluantur, sicut nec extra arcam Noe nullus potuit saluari.

Circa secundum sciendum est quod est etiam aliqua congregatio, sed malignantium, de qua Ps. "Odiui ecclesiam malignantium".
Sed hec est mala, Ecclesia uero Christi sancta: Cor.iv "Templum Dei
sanctum est" etc.; et ideo dicitur 'Sanctam Ecclesiam'.

Sanctificantur autem fideles huius congregationis ex tribus.

Primo enim quia sicut cum ecclesia consecratur, lauatur ita et
fideles loti sunt sanguine Christi: Apostolus "Viri diligite uxores
uestras" etc.; "Ecclesiam gloriosam" etc.; Hebr. "Ihesus autem ut sanc-
tificaret per sanguinem suum" etc.

Secundo ecclesia inungitur; sic et fideles spiritali unctione un-
guntur ut sanctificentur, alias enim non essent christiani; 'christus'
enim idem est quod unctus. Hec autem unctio est gratia Spiritus Sancti: Cor. "Qui signauit nos et unxit" etc.; Apostolus "Sanctificati estis
in uirtute Domini nostri" etc.

Tertio sanctificatur per inhabitantem Trinitatem. Nam ubicum-
que Deus habitat, ille locus sanctus est: unde 'Vere locus iste sanctus
est' etc., Ps. "Domum tuam, Domine, decet" etc.

Quarto, per inuocationem Dei: Ier. "Tu in nobis es, Domine, et
nomen tuum" etc. Cauendum est ergo ne post talem sanctificationem

they may be one, [just as we are one]" (John [17:22]).[54] A love of this kind, however, is manifest when the members [of the church] are solicitous one for the other, and when they are compassionate toward one another: from Christ "the whole body, joined and connected [through every joint that it was supplied, from the capacity of each and every member, makes for the growth of the body in the building up of itself in charity]" (Eph. [4:16]). Whether by office or by gift [of grace], we should all be at the service of others. Do note, however, that no one ought to make light of being put out from this church, because there is no church in which humankind is saved but this one, just as no one outside the ark of Noah was able to be saved.

(2) As to the second characteristic [of the church], we should know that there is another congregation, but of malefactors, about which the Psalm says: "I have hated the congregation of the evildoers, [and I will not sit down with the wicked]" [25:5]. However, this congregation is evil, whereas the church of Christ is holy: "[If anyone should violate the temple of God, God will destroy him,] for the temple of God is holy, [which you are]" and so forth (1 Cor. 4 [3:17]). And thus it is said [in the creed], "holy church."

The faithful of this congregation are made holy in three ways. (2.1) Just as the church is cleansed and consecrated, so the faithful are washed in the blood of Christ.[55] Paul writes: "Husbands, love your wives, [as Christ loved the church, and handed himself over for her]" and so forth, [that he might present to himself] the church glorious [and without stain] and so forth [Eph. 5:25, 27]. And "[On account of which] Jesus [suffered outside the gates,] so that he might sanctify [the people] through his own blood" and so forth (Heb. [13:12]).

(2.2) The church is anointed.[56] Similarly, the faithful are anointed by a spiritual anointing that they become holy [baptism]; otherwise they would not be Christians. Indeed, the word *christus* means "anointed." This anointing, however, is the grace of the Holy Spirit: "[It is God] who confirms us with you in Christ and who anoints us" and so forth (2 Cor. [1:21]). And Paul writes: "[And this some of you were. But you have been washed], and you have been made holy, [and you have been justified] in the name of Our Lord Jesus Christ, [and in the Spirit of our God]" and so forth [1 Cor. 6:11].[57]

(2.3) The church is made holy through the indwelling of the Trinity. Indeed, wherever God dwells, that place is holy. Thus "Truly this place is holy" and so forth [Gen. 28:17]. And "[Holiness] befits your house, O Lord [for length of days]" and so forth (Ps. [92:5]).

(2.4) The church is holy through calling upon God: "But you, O Lord, are in the midst of us, and your name [is invoked upon us;

polluamus animam, que est templum Dei, per peccatum: Apostolus "Nescitis quia templum Dei estis" etc.: "si quis templum Dei uiolauerit" etc.

Quantum ad tertium, sciendum quod Ecclesia est catholica, id est uniuersalis. Et primo quantum ad locum, quia per totum mundum, contra Donatistas; nam Ecclesia est congregatio fidelium, fideles sunt per totum mundum, ergo et Ecclesia: Ro. i "Fides nostra annuntiatur in uniuerso mundo"; Marc. "Euntes in mundum uniuersum" etc. Antiquitus autem Deus erat notus in Iudea tantum, nunc per totum mundum. Habet autem tres partes hec Ecclesia: una est in terra, alia in celo, tertia in purgatorio.

Secundo est uniuersalis quantum ad conditiones hominum, quia nullus abicitur, nec dominus nec seruus, nec masculus nec femina; nulla est in hiis differentia. Eph. "In Christo Ihesu, non est masculus".

Tertio est uniuersalis quantum ad tempus. Nam aliqui dixerunt quod Ecclesia debet durare usque ad certum tempus; sed hoc est falsum, quia hec Ecclesia incepit a tempore Abel et durabit usque ad finem mundi: Matth. "Ecce ego uobiscum sum" etc. Et post consummationem mundi remanebit in celo.

Quantum ad quartum, sciendum est quod est firma. Dicitur autem domus firma, primo si habet bona fundamenta. Principale fundamentum huius Ecclesie est Christus: Cor. "Fundamentum aliud nemo ponere potest" etc. Secundaria uero sunt apostoli et eorum doctrina, et ideo firma est; unde in Apoc. dicitur quod ciuitas habebat duodecim fundamenta, et erant ibi scripta "nomina duodecim apostolorum". Et inde est quod dicitur etiam Ecclesia apostolica; inde est quod ad designandum firmitatem huius Ecclesie, uertex Ecclesie uocatus est Petrus.

do not desert us]" and so forth (Jer. [14:9]). Therefore we should be careful, lest after such a sanctification we soil through sin our soul, which is the temple of God. Paul writes: "Do you not know that you are the temple of God, [and the Spirit of God dwells in you?] and so forth. But if anyone violate the temple of God, [God will destroy him]" and so forth [1 Cor. 3:16–17].

(3) As to the third characteristic, we should know that the church is catholic, i.e., universal.

(3.1) First of all, it is catholic with regard to place, because [it extends] throughout the whole world (in opposition to what the Donatists[58] say). After all, the church is the congregation of the faithful, and inasmuch as the faithful are found throughout the whole world, so is the church: "[First of all, I give thanks to my God through Jesus Christ for all of you, because] your faith is proclaimed in all the world" (Rom. [1:8]). And "Going into the whole world, [preach the Good News to every creature]" and so forth (Mark [16:15]). In ancient times, God was known in Judaea alone, but now God is known throughout the whole world. This church, however, has three divisions: one on earth, another in heaven, and a third in purgatory.

(3.2) The church is universal with regard to the human condition, because no one is rejected, neither lord nor servant, neither male nor female. There is no difference among them [with regard to the human condition]: "[There is neither Jew nor Greek, neither slave nor free,] neither male [nor female; all of you are one] in Christ Jesus" (Eph. [Gal. 3:28]).

(3.3) The church is universal with regard to time. Some have said that the church should endure just for a certain time. But this is false, because the church began from the time of Abel and will perdure until the end of the world: "And behold I am with you [all days, even unto the consummation of the ages]" and so forth (Mt. [28:20]). And after the consummation of the world, it [the church] will remain in heaven.

(4) As to the fourth characteristic, we should know that the church is perduring. A house is said to be lasting if in the first place it has good foundations. The main foundation of this church is Christ: "No one can lay another foundation, [beside the one which has been laid down, which is Christ Jesus]" and so forth (1 Cor. [3:11]). The apostles and their teaching are the secondary foundations, and thus the church is perduring. In the Apocalypse we read that the city [the heavenly city of Jerusalem] had twelve foundations, "and the names of the twelve apostles" were written there [21:14]. Thus the church is also called apostolic. And to designate the perdurance of this church, Peter[59] is called the pinnacle of the church.

Apparet autem firmitas eius quia nullo modo potuit destrui a persecutoribus. Immo in persecutionibus magis creuit, quia siue alii persequerentur eam, deficiebant; si uero Ecclesia persequatur aliquos, deficiunt, iuxta illud "Qui ceciderit super lapidem istum, confringetur; super quem uero" etc. Non ab erroribus: immo quanto magis errores superuenerunt, tanto magis ueritas manifesta est. Thi. "Homines reprobi mente, corrupti" etc. Non a temptationibus demonum: Ecclesia enim est sicut turris ad quam quicumque pugnat contra dyabolum, confugit; Prou. "Turris fortissima nomen Domini" etc. Et ideo dyabolus precipue conatur ad destructionem illius; sed non preualet, quia Dominus dixit "Et porte inferi" etc., quasi dicat "Bellabunt aduersus te et non preualebunt".

Et inde est quod sola Ecclesia Petri semper fuit firma in fide aliorum apostolorum, cum in omnibus aliis fides uel nulla sit, uel admixta erroribus; Ecclesia uero Petri et fide uiget et ab erroribus munda est: nec mirum, quia Dominus dixit Petro "Ego pro te rogaui, Petre" etc.

The church's perdurance is apparent, because persecutors were in no way able to destroy it. Moreover, in persecution the church grew the more, because those who persecuted her failed, and even those the church persecuted [opposed] failed, according to the text: "And whoever falls upon this stone will be shattered, but [it will crush] the one upon whom [it falls]" and so forth [Mt. 21:44]. Nor by errors. Especially as errors came over her, so much the more was the truth manifested: "[Jannes and Mambres were opposed to Moses, and so these men are opposed to the truth:] men corrupt in mind, unexamined in their faith.⁶⁰ [But they will not succeed very far; their stupidity will be manifest to everyone, just as those men mentioned above]" and so forth (2 Tim. [3:8–9]). Nor the temptations of the demons. The church is like a tower to which whosoever combats the devil can flee: "The name of the Lord is a fortified tower; [the just man runs to it, and he is lifted up]" and so forth (Prov. [18:10]). Therefore, the devil especially strives for the destruction of this church, but he shall not prevail, because the Lord said: "[You are Peter, and upon this rock I will build my church,] and the gates of hell [shall not prevail against her]" and so forth [Mt. 16:18]. In effect the Lord said: "They will make war against you, but they will not win."

Thus it is that only the church of Peter has always been perduring in the faith of the other apostles [apostolic faith]. In all the others, there is either no faith or a faith mixed with errors. But the church of Peter both flourishes in faith and is cleansed from errors. No need to wonder, because the Lord said to Peter: "I have prayed for you, Peter [that your faith may not be lacking, and that when you are converted, you might confirm your brethren]" and so forth [Luke 22:32].

This division of the Aquinas commentary concerns the meaning of the "communion of saints and the forgiveness of sins." From a consideration of the church as the body of Christ, and the Christian as a member of this body of which Christ is the head, Aquinas draws the traditional conclusion that the graces of Christ are shared in the church through the sacraments. Hence the great evil of excommunication, which separates the Christian from all the goods of the church in Christ. Aquinas's treatment of the sacraments is in brief outline form. He speaks more at length in his "De Articulis Fidei," which is a somewhat earlier commentary on the creed.

His remarks about marriage will put off the contemporary reader. Viewing marriage from a nonromantic point of view, he concludes that marriage is useful in order to be saved and to use human sexuality without serious sin. The perspective of reason on human passion even within marriage was austere from the Patristic period into the Middle Ages.

Sanctorum communionem, remissionem peccatorum.

Sicut in corpore naturali operatio unius membri cedit in bonum totius corporis, ita in corpore spirituali, scilicet Ecclesia. Et ideo, quia omnes fideles sunt unum corpus, ideo bonum unius communicatur alteri. Apostolus "Singuli alter alterius membra". Vnde et inter alia que apostoli credenda tradiderunt, est quod communio bonorum sit in Ecclesia: et hoc est quod dicitur 'Sanctorum communionem'.

Inter alia autem membra Ecclesie principale membrum est Christus; nam ipse est caput Ecclesie: Eph. "Et ipsum dedit caput super omnem Ecclesiam que est corpus eius". Bonum ergo Christi communicatur omnibus christianis, sicut uirtus capitis communicatur omnibus membris; et hec communio fit per sacramenta Ecclesie, in quibus operatur uirtus passionis Christi ad conferendum gratiam et ad remissionem peccatorum.

Huiusmodi autem sacramenta sunt septem. Primum est baptismus, qui est quedam regeneratio spiritualis. Sicut enim uita carnalis non potest haberi nisi homo carnaliter nascatur, ita et uita spiritualis haberi non potest nisi homo renascatur spiritualiter; et hec regeneratio fit per baptismum. Io. "Nisi quis renatus fuerit" etc. Et sciendum quod sicut homo non nascitur corporaliter nisi semel, sic semel tantum baptizatur; et ideo sancti addiderunt in alio symbolo 'Confiteor unum baptisma'.

Est ergo uirtus baptismi quod purgat ab omnibus peccatis, et quantum ad penam et quantum ad culpam; et inde est quod nulla penitentia imponitur baptizatis quantumcumque fuerint peccatores, et si moriuntur post baptismum, statim euolant. Inde est etiam quod,

Communion of saints, forgiveness of sins.

Just as in a physical body the operation of one member redounds to the good of the whole body, so it works in a spiritual body, that is to say, in the church. Since all the faithful are one body, the good of one is communicated to another. Paul writes: "[Thus, we who are many are one body in Christ,] individuals, yet members one of the other" [Rom. 12:5]. Thus, among other matters which should be believed that the apostles handed down, there remains the communion of goods in the church. This [doctrine] is called "the communion of saints."

Among all the other members of the church, however, the principal member is Christ, for he is the head of the church: "[And he put down everything under his feet, and] he put himself as head over the whole church, which is his body, [the fullness of him who fulfills everything in everyone]" (Eph. [1:22–23]). Therefore the good of Christ is communicated to all Christians, as the wisdom of the head is communicated to all the members. This communion comes about through the sacraments of the church, in which the strength of the passion of Christ for conferring grace and for forgiving sins operates.

These sacraments, however, are seven. (1) The first is baptism, which is a certain spiritual rebirth. Just as carnal life cannot be had unless a human being is born carnally, so spiritual life cannot be had unless one is reborn spiritually. And this rebirth comes about through baptism: "[Jesus replied: 'Amen, amen I say to you,] unless one would be reborn [from water and from the Holy Spirit, one is unable to enter the kingdom of God']" and so forth (John [3:5]). And just as we grant that a human being is born bodily only once, so only once is he or she baptized. Therefore the holy fathers added in the other symbol [the Niceno-Constantinopolitan Creed]: "I confess one baptism [for the forgiveness of sins]."

It is therefore the power of baptism that cleanses from all sins, both as to the punishment and as to the guilt. Thus, no penance is imposed on those baptized, howsoever much they were sinners. And if they were to die after baptism, they would immediately ascend [to

135

licet ex officio soli sacerdotes baptizent, ex necessitate tamen cuilibet licet baptizare, seruata tamen forma baptismi que est 'Ego te bap-
tizo' etc.

Sumit etiam hoc sacramentum uirtutem ex passione Christi: Ro.
"Quicumque enim baptizati sumus in morte" etc. Et inde est quod
sicut Christus fuit tribus diebus in sepulcro, ita fit triplex immersio
in aqua.

Secundum est confirmatio. Sicut enim illis qui naturaliter
nascuntur necessarie sunt uires ad operandum, sic spiritualiter re-
natis necessarium est robur Spiritus Sancti; unde et apostoli ad hoc
quod essent fortes receperunt Spiritum Sanctum post ascensionem
Christi: Act. "Sedete hic in ciuitate" etc. Hoc autem robur confertur
in sacramento confirmationis; et ideo illi qui curam habent puerorum diligenter studere debent quod pueri confirmentur, quia in con-
firmatione confertur magna gratia; et si decedat, maiorem gloriam
habet quam non confirmatus, quia hic habuit plus de gratia.

Tertium est eucharistia. Sicut enim in uita corporali, postquam
homo natus est et uires sumpsit, necessarius est cibus ut conserue-
tur et sustentetur; ita in uita spirituali, post robur necessarius est cibus spiritualis qui est corpus Christi. Io. "Nisi manducaueritis carnem" etc. Et inde est quod, secundum ordinem Ecclesie, semel in anno
quilibet christianus debet recipere corpus Christi; munde tamen et
digne, quia "Qui manducat et bibit indigne", scilicet cum conscientia
peccati mortalis de quo non est confessus, uel non proponit abstinere,
"iudicium sibi manducat et bibit".

Quartum est penitentia. Contingit enim quod in uita corporali
quis infirmatur, et nisi habeat medicinam moritur; ita in uita spirituali quis infirmatur per peccatum, unde ad sanitatem recuperandam
est necessaria medicina: et hec est gratia que confertur in sacramento penitentie. Ps. "Qui propitiatur omnibus iniquitatibus tuis, qui
sanat" etc. Debent esse autem tria in penitentia: contritio que est dolor

heaven]. Thus it also is that although by office only priests may baptize, nevertheless by necessity anyone at all is allowed to baptize, provided the form of baptism is observed: "I baptize you [in the name of the Father, and of the Son, and of the Holy Spirit]" and so forth.

This sacrament takes its strength from the passion of Christ: "[Could you be ignorant that] whoever is baptized [in Christ Jesus, is baptized] in his death?" and so forth (Rom [6:3]). Thus, just as Christ was three days in the tomb, so there is a threefold immersion in the water.

(2) Confirmation. Just as those who are naturally born must have energy for doing, so the spiritually reborn must have the vigor of the Holy Spirit. Thus the apostles received the Holy Spirit after the ascension of Christ so that they might be strengthened: "[And I am sending the promised one of my Father unto you; but] stay put in the city, [until you are clothed with power from on high]" and so forth (Acts [Luke 24:49]). This vigor, however, is conferred in the sacrament of confirmation. Thus, those who have care of youth ought to strive diligently that these youth may be confirmed, because in confirmation a great grace is conferred. If one [confirmed] were to die, he or she would have greater glory than one who was not confirmed, because the former has received more grace.

(3) The Eucharist. In bodily life, after human beings are born and gain their powers, food is required so that it might conserve and sustain them. So it goes in the spiritual life; after the strengthening [of confirmation] spiritual food, which is the body of Christ, is required: "[Jesus said to them: 'Amen, amen I say to you:] unless you shall have eaten the flesh [of the Son of man, and drunk his blood, you will not have life in you']" and so forth (John [6:54]). Thus it is, following the [liturgical] order of the church, once a year each and every Christian ought to receive the body of Christ. Nonetheless, it should be received conscientiously and worthily, because "whoever eats and drinks unworthily" [1 Cor. 11:29], that is to say, with a conscience of mortal sin which has not been confessed, or from which there is no intention to refrain, "eats and drinks judgment upon himself [not discerning the body of the Lord]" [1 Cor. 11:29].

(4) Penance. In bodily life it may happen that one becomes sick, and unless given medicine, dies. Similarly, in the spiritual life, one becomes ill through sin, and then medicine is necessary for recovering one's health. This [medicine] is the grace conferred in the sacrament of penance: "Who atones for all your iniquities, and heals [all your infirmities]" and so forth (Ps. [102:3]). In the sacrament of penance three conditions are required: contrition that is sorrow for sin

de peccato cum proposito abstinendi, confessio omnium peccatorum cum integritate, et satisfactio per bona opera.

Quintum est extrema unctio. In hac enim uita sunt multa que impediunt quod non potest homo perfecte per penitentiam consequi purgationem a peccatis; et quia nullus potest intrare uitam eternam nisi sit bene purgatus, necessarium fuit aliud sacramentum quo homo purgetur, liberetur ab infirmitate et preparetur ad introitum celestis regni: et hoc est sacramentum extreme unctionis. Et hoc non semper curat corporaliter, quia forte non expedit anime infirmi: Iac. "Et si in peccatis fuerit, dimittuntur ei".

Sic ergo sunt quinque sacramenta per que habetur perfectio uite. Sed quia necessarium est quod hec sacramenta ministrentur per determinatos ministros, ideo necessarium fuit sacramentum ordinis, cuius ministerio huiusmodi sacramenta dispensarentur. Nec est in hoc attendenda eorum uita, sed uirtus Christi per quam ipsa sacramenta efficaciam habent: Cor. "Sic nos existimet homo" etc. Et hoc est sextum sacramentum.

Septimum est matrimonium, in quo, si coniunguntur munde, homines saluantur et possunt sine peccato mortali uiuere.

Per hec autem septem sacramenta consequimur remissionem peccatorum, et ideo sequitur 'Remissionem peccatorum'. Per hoc etiam datum est apostolis dimittere peccata; et ideo credendum est quod ministri Ecclesie potestatem habent soluendi, et quod in Ecclesia sit plena potestas dimittendi peccata.

Sciendum est autem quod non solum uirtus passionis Christi communicatur nobis, sed etiam meritum uite Christi; et quicquid boni fecerunt omnes sancti communicatur hiis qui in caritate uiuunt, quia omnes unum sunt. Ps. "Particeps ego sum omnium timentium te". Et inde est quod qui in caritate uiuit, particeps est omnis boni quod fit in toto mundo, sed tamen specialius illi pro quibus specialiter fit aliquod bonum; nam unus potest satisfacere pro alio, sicut patet in beneficiis ad que plures congregationes admittunt aliquos.

with the intention of abstaining from sin; confession of all one's sins with integrity; and satisfaction through good works.

(5) Extreme Unction. In this life there are many things that impede us, so that one cannot perfectly attain through penance the cleansing of our sins. And because no one can enter eternal life unless he or she is well cleansed [of sins], another sacrament was necessary in order that one might be cleansed, freed from sickness, and prepared for entrance into the heavenly kingdom. This sacrament is extreme unction. It does not always cure in a bodily way, because it does not perhaps benefit the soul of the sick person: "[Is anyone ill among you? Let him call in the elders of the church, and let them pray over him, anointing him with oil in the name of the Lord. The prayer of faith will save the sick person; the Lord will alleviate his illness,] and if he has committed sins, they will be taken away from him" (Jas. [5: 14–15]).

(6) So there remain five sacraments through which the perfection of life is obtained. But, because these sacraments must be administered through designated ministers, the sacrament of orders was required, so that by the ministry of one ordained the sacraments might be dispensed. Their [moral] life need not be factored in this [distribution of the sacraments], for these sacraments owe their efficacy to the power of Christ: "So, let everyone consider us [ministers of Christ and dispensers of the mysteries of God]" and so forth (1 Cor. [4:1]). And this is the sixth sacrament.

(7) The seventh sacrament is matrimony, in which, if they are properly wedded, men and women are saved and enabled to live without mortal sin.

Through these seven sacraments we accomplish the forgiveness of sins, and therefore "the forgiveness of sins" [in the creed] follows [the communion of saints]. Consequently, the apostles were also enabled to forgive sins. We must believe that the ministers of the church have the power of absolving [sins], and that in the church there is full power to forgive sins.

We should know that not only the strength of the passion of Christ is communicated to us, but also the merit of the life of Christ. Whatever good all the saints might accomplish is communicated to those who live in charity, because all of us are one: "I am a partaker with all those who fear you [and who keep your commandments]" (Ps. [118:63]). Thus it is that whoever lives in charity participates in all the good that goes on in the whole world. However, such participation more especially extends to the person for whom the good is especially done, because one man can satisfy for another, as is evident in the benefits which many congregations extend to others.

Sic ergo duo habemus per hanc communionem: unum, quod meritum passionis Christi communicatur omnibus; aliud, quod bonum unius communicatur alteri. Vnde excommunicati hoc perdunt et partem omnium honorum que fiunt, quod est maius dampnum quam alicuius rei temporalis. Est etiam aliud periculum, quia constat quod per suffragia impeditur dyabolus quod non potest temptare; unde quando excluditur aliquis ab huiusmodi suffragiis, facilius dyabolus uincit eum. Et inde est quod in primitiua Ecclesia statim cum quis excommunicabatur, dyabolus uexabat eum corporaliter.

Rogemus Dominum etc.

Two benefits emerge from this communion [of saints]. (1) The merit of the passion of Christ is communicated to everyone. (2) The good of one person is communicated to another. Thus, those excommunicated lose this and a share of all the good that goes on, which is a greater loss than the loss of any temporal good. There is also another danger. Given that through suffrages [prayers for others] the devil is impeded so that he cannot tempt [them], when anyone is excluded from suffrages of this kind, the devil more easily conquers them. Thus, in the early church, when anyone was excommunicated, the devil immediately tormented them bodily.

Let us pray to the Lord, and so forth.

This division of the Aquinas commentary concerns the meaning of the "resurrection of the body." Hope of the resurrection of our bodies gives us consolation when our loved ones die, and also protects us from a boundless fear of our own death.

Of particular interest are the notes of the resurrected body that Aquinas tries rationally to describe. The human body will be: (1) the same body somehow; (2) an immortal body that will die no more; (3) an integral body without defect; (4) a mature body, for which Aquinas suggests the optimal age of thirty-three years [the age at which Christ is thought to have died]. In addition, the blessed will have a body that will boast: (1) clarity and light in its flesh; (2) invulnerability to pain and death; (3) agility [think of the condition of weightlessness in contemporary space probes]; and (4) spiritual transparency.

Carnis resurrectionem.

Spiritus Sanctus non solum sanctificat Ecclesiam quantum ad animam, sed etiam uirtute eius corpora nostra resurgent: Ro. "Qui suscitauit Ihesum Christum a mortuis" etc.; "per hominem resurrectio mortuorum". Et ideo credimus secundum fidem nostram resurrectionem mortuorum futuram.

Circa quam quatuor consideranda occurrunt: primum est utilitas que ex fide resurrectionis prouenit; secundum est qualitas resurgentium quantum ad omnes in generali; tertium quantum ad bonos et quartum quantum ad malos, in speciali.

Circa primum sciendum est quod ad quatuor est utilis nobis spes resurrectionis et fides. Primo ad tollendas tristitias quas ex mortuis concipimus: impossibile est enim quod homo non doleat de morte amici; sed per hoc quod sperat eum resurrecturum, multum temperatur dolor mortis. Machab. "Nolumus uos ignorare" etc.

Secundo aufert timorem mortis. Nam si homo post mortem non speraret aliam uitam meliorem, sine dubio mors esset ualde timenda, et potius deberet homo quecumque mala facere quam incurrere mortem. Sed quia credimus esse aliam meliorem uitam ad quam perueniemus post mortem, constat quod nullus debet timere mortem, nec propter timorem mortis aliquod peccatum facere. Hebr. "Vt per mortem destrueret eum qui habebat" etc.

Tertio reddit sollicitos et studiosos ad bene operandum. Si enim uita hominis esset tantum ista qua uiuimus, non inesset hominibus magnum studium ad bene operandum; quia quicquid faceret paruum esset, cum desiderium eius non sit ad bonum determinatum secundum certum tempus, sed ad eternitatem. Sed quia credimus quod per

The resurrection of the flesh.

The Holy Spirit not only sanctifies the church with regard to its soul, but by its power our bodies will arise: "[to those believing in him] who raised up Jesus Christ Our Lord from the dead" and so forth (Rom. [4:24]). And "[Because just as through a human being death came about, so] through a human being the resurrection from the dead" (1 Cor. [15:21]). Therefore we believe according to our faith in the future resurrection of the dead.

About this [resurrection] there are four thoughts that should be considered: (1) the usefulness that comes from faith in the resurrection; (2) the quality [of life] of those who arise with regard to everyone in general; (3) with regard to good men and women in particular, and (4) with regard to evil men and women in particular.

(1) About the first, we should know that faith and hope in the resurrection is helpful to us for four reasons: (1.1) It takes away the sadness which we bear for those who died. It is impossible that someone not grieve over the death of a friend; yet, insofar as they hope their friend will arise, the sorrow of death is much assuaged: "We do not wish you to be ignorant of" and so forth (Mac.).[61]

(1.2) [The resurrection of the flesh] takes away the fear of death. If a human being were not to hope in another and better life after death, without doubt death would be excessively feared. One would rather have to do any evil deed than to incur death. But, because we believe there is another and better life to which we shall attain after death, it stands that no one ought to fear death, nor commit any sin on account of the fear of death: "that through death he might destroy him who had [the empire of death, that is, the devil]" and so forth (Heb. [2:14]).

(1.3) [The resurrection of the flesh] renders us solicitous and studious for behaving well. If the life of a human being were only what we now experience, there would not be any great effort among humankind for behaving well. Whatever a human being would do might seem trivial, since it would be a determinate good measured in time, rather than in eternity.[62] However, since we believe that through

145

hec que hic facimus, recipiemus bona eterna in resurrectione, ideo studemus bona operari: Cor. "Si in hac uita tantum sperantes essemus" etc.

Quarto retrahit a malo. Sicut enim spes premii allicit ad bene operandum, ita timor pene quam credimus malis reseruari, retrahit a malo. Matth. Resurgent hii "in resurrectionem uite" etc.

Circa secundum sciendum est quod, quantum ad omnes quadruplex conditio attendi potest in resurrectione. Prima conditio est quantum ad idemptitatem corporum resurgentium: quia idem corpus quod nunc est et quantum ad carnem et quantum ad ossa resurget, licet aliqui dixerint quod non hoc corpus quod nunc corrumpitur resurget. Quod falsum est, quia sacra Scriptura dicit quod uirtute Dei idem corpus resurget ad uitam. Iob "Rursum circumdabor pelle mea" etc.

Secunda conditio est quantum ad qualitatem, quia corpora resurgentia erunt alterius qualitatis quam nunc sint. Quia etiam quantum ad bonos et quantum ad malos corpora erunt incorruptibilia, quia boni erunt semper in gloria, mali uero semper in pena. Cor. "Oportet corruptibile hoc" etc. Et quia corpus erit incorruptibile et immortale, ideo post resurrectionem non erit usus ciborum nec uenereorum: Matth. "In resurrectione uero, neque nubent" etc. Et hoc est contra Saracenos et Iudeos. Iob "Non reuertetur ultra in domum suam" etc.

Tertia conditio est quantum ad integritatem, quia omnes boni et mali resurgent in omni integritate que est ad perfectionem hominis; quia non erit claudus nec cecus, nec aliquis defectus: Thess. "Mortui resurgent incorrupti".

Quarta conditio est quantum ad etatem, quia omnes resurgent in etate perfecta, id est triginta trium annorum seu duorum. Cuius

this [resurrection of the flesh] we will receive eternal goods in the resurrection for what we do here and now, we will strive to lead a good life: "If in only this life we are people hoping [in Christ, we are more pitiable than everybody else]" and so forth (1 Cor. [15:19]).

(1.4) The [resurrection of the flesh] draws us away from evil. Just as the hope of a reward entices [us] to live well, so fear of pain that we believe is reserved for the wicked, draws us away from evil: These will rise up, "[and those who accomplished good things will enter into] the resurrection of life; [those who worked evil into the resurrection of judgment]" and so forth (Mt. [John 5:29]).

(2) We should know that with regard to everyone [in general] a fourfold condition in the resurrection can be noted.

(2.1) With regard to the identity of the bodies of those who arise. The same body that now exists, both in its flesh and in its bones, will rise, although some will say that not this body which is now corrupted will rise. This is false, because sacred Scripture says that by the power of God the same body will rise to life: "And once my skin has been undone, [I will see my God once more in my flesh]" and so forth (Job [19:26]).

(2.2) With regard to the condition [of those who rise]. The risen bodies will be in another condition than they now are. With regard to good men and women [in particular] and evil men and women [in particular] their bodies will be incorruptible, because the good will always be in glory, but the evil [will be] always in pain: "This corruptible nature must [clothe itself with incorruption, and this mortal nature clothe itself with immortality]" and so forth (1 Cor. [15:53]). And because the body will be immortal and incorruptible, there will be no use for food or sex after the resurrection: "In the resurrection they will neither marry [nor be married; but they will be as the angels of God in heaven]" and so forth (Mt. [22:30]). The Saracens [Muslims] and the Jews hold to the contrary.[63] But we read in Job: "He will no longer go back into his home, [nor will his place know him any further]" and so forth [7:10].

(2.3) With regard to the integrity [of those who rise in the flesh]. All the good people and all the evil people will rise in all their integrity which belongs to the perfection of humankind. There will be no deafness nor blindness, nor anyone defective: "[In a moment, in the blink of an eye, in the last sounds of the trumpet; the trumpet will sing, and] the dead will rise up incorruptible, [and we will be changed]" (Thess. [1 Cor. 15:52]).

(2.4) With regard to age [of those who rise in the flesh.] Everyone will rise in a perfect state, i.e., thirty-two or thirty-three years of age.

ratio est, quia qui nondum peruenerunt ad hoc non habent etatem perfectam, et senes iam amiserunt; et ideo iuuenibus et pueris addetur, senibus uero restituetur: Cor. "Donec occurramus" etc.

Circa tertium sciendum est, quantum ad bonos erit specialis gloria, quia sancti habebunt corpora glorificata in quibus erit quadruplex conditio. Prima est claritas: Matth. "Fulgebunt iusti" etc.; secunda, impassibilitas: Cor. "Seminatur in corruptione" etc.; Apoc. "Absterget Deus" etc. Tertia est agilitas: Sap. "Fulgebunt iusti" etc. Quarta est subtilitas: Cor. "Seminatur corpus animale"; non quod sit omnino spiritus, sed quia erit totaliter spiritui subiectum.

Circa quartum sciendum est quod dampnatorum conditio erit contraria conditioni bonorum, quia erit eis eterna pena. In qua est quadruplex mala conditio. Nam primo corpora erunt obscura: Ysa. "Facies combuste uultus eorum". Secundo erunt passibilia, quia semper in igne: Ysa. "Vermis eorum non morietur" etc. Tertio erunt grauia; ibi enim erit anima quasi cathenata grauedine corporum: Ps. "Ad alligandos reges eorum" etc. Quarto erunt carnalia et anima et corpus: Ioel "Computrescent iumenta" etc.

Rogemus Dominum etc.

The reason is because those who have not yet come to this [age] have not achieved a perfect state, and older people already have lost it. Therefore to children and to youth [age] is added, but to old folks it is restored: "Until we all attain [to the unity of faith, and the recognition of the Son of God, to perfect manhood, to the measure of the stature of the fullness of Christ]" and so forth (Cor. [Eph. 4:13]).

(3) We should know that with regard to good people, there will be a special glory, because the saints will have glorified bodies in which a fourfold condition will obtain.

(3.1) Clarity: "[Then] the just will shine [like the sun in the kingdom of their Father]" and so forth (Mt. [13:43]).

(3.2) Invulnerability: "What is sown in deterioration, [will rise up in glory. What is sown in weakness, will rise up in strength]" and so forth (1 Cor. [15:43]). And, "God will dry [every tear from their eyes, and death will be no more, nor mourning, nor weeping, nor will there be any more sorrow, because the former things have passed away]" and so forth (Apoc. [21:4]).

(3.3) Agility: "The just will shine forth, [and they will leap forth like sparks in tinder]" and so forth (Wis. [3.7]).

(3.4) Soulfulness: "An animal body is sown, [a spiritual body will rise up]" (1 Cor. [15:44]). The body will not be altogether spirit, but it will be totally subject to the spirit.

(4) We should know that the condition of the damned will be the opposite of the condition of the blessed, because eternal pain will be theirs. A fourfold condition will obtain.

(4.1) [Their] bodies will be darkened: "[Pangs and sorrows will grasp them, just as a woman suffers in labor;] everyone will be astonished at their neighbor;] burnt faces their looks" (Is. [13:8]).

(4.2) [Their bodies] will be vulnerable, because always on fire: "[And they will go forth and look upon the body of those men who plotted against me;] their worm will not die, [and their fire will not be extinguished; and they will be so unto the satiation of the sight of all flesh]" and so forth (Is. [66:24]).

(4.3) [Their bodies] will be weighed down. The soul will be as if chained in the torpor of bodies: "For binding their kings [in foot-chains, and their nobles in iron manacles]" and so forth (Ps. [149:8]).

(4.4) They will be carnal, both in body and in soul: "The barn animals rot [in their own dung; the barns are torn down; the storehouses are wasted, because the grain is not viable]" and so forth (Joel [1:17]).

Let us pray to the Lord, and so forth.

XV

This division of the Aquinas commentary concerns the meaning of "eternal life." Aquinas argues that if the soul dies, human beings are no better than brutes.

Aquinas attempts again a rational description of the conditions that will obtain in "eternal life." The blessed will enjoy union with God: (1) face to face without intermediary; (2) intense love and union with God; (3) supreme worship of God; (4) satiation of all desires, for all desires are at bottom desire for God; (5) possession of all honors desired; (6) possession of all knowing desired; (7) security against any future loss of the goods above; and (8) communal sharing of the goods.

Aquinas ends his commentary on the creed by proposing a more rational ordering of the twelve articles of the creed. He would divide the creed into two halves of six articles each, but the articles composed somewhat differently. One half of the creed would treat the divinity of Christ, and the other equal half would treat the humanity. The actual arrangement of the creed that we are accustomed to coalesced slowly and haphazardly through the passage of the centuries. The number "twelve" preserves the legend that the Apostles' Creed was written by the twelve apostles, each composing an article before their setting off on separate missions after Pentecost day. Aquinas regroups the articles of the creed in order to give it a more logical arrangement.

Vitam eternam. Amen.

Conuenienter in fine omnium desideriorum nostrorum, scilicet in uita eterna, finis datur credendis in Symbolo; et ideo dicit 'Vitam eternam amen', contra quod dicunt illi qui ponunt animam perire cum corpore: si enim hoc esset uerum, homo esset eiusdem conditionis cum brutis. Et istis conuenit illud Ps. "Homo, cum in honore esset, non intellexit" etc. Anima enim humana assimilatur Deo in immortalitate, ex parte autem sensibilitatis assimilatur bestiis; cum ergo credit quis quod anima moriatur cum corpore, recedit a Dei similitudine et bestiis comparatur: contra quos dicitur Sap. "Non sperauerunt mercedem iustitie" etc.

Est autem in hoc articulo primo considerandum que uita est uita eterna. Circa quod sciendum est quod, in uita eterna primum est quod in ea homo intime Deo coniungitur; nam ipse Deus est premium et finis omnium laborum nostrorum: Exo. "Ego Dominus, merces tua".

Consistit autem hec unio in perfecta uisione: Cor. "Videmus nunc per speculum" etc.; in feruentissimo amore, quanto enim aliquis cognoscitur, plus amatur; in summa laude, Augustinus "Videbimus, et amabimus, et laudabimus" etc.; Ysa. "Gaudium et letitiam" etc.

Secundo est in ea plena et perfecta satietas desiderii: nam ibi habebit quilibet beatus sua desiderata et sperata. Cuius ratio est quia nichil potest in uita ista implere desiderium, nec unquam aliquid creatum satiat desiderium hominis; Deus autem solus satiat, qui in

Eternal life. Amen.

Fittingly, with the end of all our desires, that is to say, with eternal life, an end is given to those matters to be believed in the Symbol [the creed]. Thus we read: "eternal life. Amen." This stands against those who say the soul perishes with the body. If that were true, a human being would be in the same condition as brute animals. Against these [objectors] the Psalm argues: "A human being does not understand when he is held in honor; [he is to be compared with the dumb beasts of the field, and he makes himself like them]" and so forth [48:21]. The human soul in its immortality resembles God, whereas in its sensibility it resembles the animals. Therefore, when anyone believes that the soul dies with the body, they fall away from the likeness to God and are compared to the animals. In opposition Wisdom says: "[And they did not know the mysteries of God,] nor did they hope for a reward for justice, [nor did they weigh the high state of holy souls]" and so forth [2:22].

(1.1) In this article the first thing that should be considered is life eternal. In this regard we should know that eternal life first of all consists in this, that a human being is intimately espoused to God. Indeed, God is the reward and end of all our labors: "I, the Lord, am your reward" (Ex. [2:9]).[64]

This union, however, consists in perfect vision [of God]: "Now we see through a mirror [in symbols, but then we shall see face to face]" and so forth (1 Cor. [13:12]). This union consists in a most intense love, for the more one knows, the more one loves. And this union consists in supreme worship. Augustine writes: "We will see, and we will love, and we will praise" and so forth.[65] And, "[the Lord will console Zion, and all her ruins; he will make her desert like a garden of the Lord]. Joy and celebration [will be found within her, and thanksgiving and the sound of praise]" and so forth (Is. [51:3]).

(1.2) In eternal life there is full and perfect satiation of desire. Each and every blessed one will have there fulfilled his or her own desires and hopes. The reason is that nothing in this life can fill our desire, nor any creature ever satiate the desire of a human being. God

infinitum excedit. Et inde est quod non quiescit nisi in Deo: Augustinus "Fecisti nos, Domine, ad te" etc. Vnde, quia in patria sancti habebunt perfecte Deum, cum sit ipse premium nostrum, manifestum est quod satiabitur desiderium nostrum; et adhuc excedit gloria, et ideo dicit Dominus "Intra in gaudium Domini tui".[10] Ideo dicebat Dauid "Satiabor cum apparuerit" etc.; inde etiam est quod dicitur "Qui replet in bonis desiderium" etc.

Quicquid enim desiderabile est, totum est ibi superhabundanter. Si enim appetuntur delectationes, ibi erit summa et perfectissima delectatio, quia de summo bono, scilicet de Deo. Iob "Tunc super omnipotente deliciis afflues".

Si appetuntur honores, ibi erit omnis honor. Homines enim potissime desiderant esse reges quantum ad laicos, et episcopi quantum ad clericos; et hoc erit ibi: Apoc. "Fecisti nos Deo nostro regnum et sacerdotes"; Sap. "Ecce computati sunt inter filios Dei" etc.

Si appetitur scientia, ibi erit perfectissima. Quia omnes naturas rerum, omnem ueritatem et quicquid uolumus scire, sciemus ibi; et quicquid uoluerimus habere, habebimus ibi cum ipsa uita eterna. Sap. "Venerunt michi omnia bona" etc.; Prou. "Desiderium suum iustis dabitur".

Tertio est perfectissima securitas. Nam in mundo isto non est securitas plena, quia quanto plus habet quis et quanto magis preminet, tanto plura timet et pluribus indiget; sed in uita eterna nulla tristitia, nullus labor, nullus timor: Prou. "Habundantia perfruetur" etc.

Quarto est ibi omnimoda societas omnium bonorum, que quidem societas est maxime delectabilis bonis. Sic ergo habebunt omnia bona cum omnibus bonis, et quilibet diliget ibi alium sicut se ipsum; et ita gaudebit de bono alterius sicut de bono suo. Quo fit ut tantum augeatur letitia et gaudium unius, quantum est gaudium omnium: Ps. "Sicut letantium omnium" etc.

alone, who surpasses infinity, satisfies [us]. And thus it is that humankind will not be at rest except in God. Augustine says: "You have made us, O Lord, for yourself" and so forth.[66] Wherefore, in our fatherland the saints perfectly possess God, since God himself is our reward. So obviously God will satisfy our desire. The glory [of God] will surpass all that went before, and therefore the Lord says, "[Well done, good and faithful servant, because you have been faithful over a few things, I will place you over many things;] enter into the joy of your Lord" [Mt. 25:21]. Thus David said: "[But I will appear in your sight in justice;] I will be satisfied when [your glory] appears" and so forth [Ps. 16:15]. And it is said, "Who fulfills with good things one's desire" and so forth [Ps. 102:5].

Whatever is desirable will be all there superabundantly. If delights are yearned for, there will be supreme and fully perfect delight, because [they come] from God who is the highest good: "Then you will abound in the delights of the Almighty, [and you will lift up your face to God]" (Job [22:26]).

If honors are yearned for, every honor will be there. People desire vehemently to be kings, if they are lay people, and to be bishops, if they are clerics. And there [in heaven] this will be: "And you have made us into priests and into a kingdom for our God, [and we will reign over the earth]" (Apoc. [5:10]). And "Behold how they are counted among the sons of God" and so forth (Wis. [5:5]).

If knowledge is yearned for, it will there be most perfect, because we will know there the nature of everything, all truth, and whatsoever we wish to know. And whatever we want to have, we shall there have it as part of life eternal: "All good things have come to me along with her" and so forth (Wis. [7:11]). And, "[What the wicked fears will come over him;] the wishes of the just will be granted" (Prov. [10:24]).

(1.3) [In life eternal] there is security most perfect. In this world there is no complete security, because the more one has and the more one stands out, so much the more does one fear and [still] lack many things. But, in eternal life there will be no sadness, no labor, no fear [of loss]. "[But whoever listens to me will rest without terror,] and will enjoy abundance, [with the fear of evils taken away]" and so forth (Prov. [1:33]).

(1.4) In heaven there will be every kind of sharing of all goods, which society is supremely delightful to good people. There all goods will be shared with all good people, and each one there will love the other as oneself. Thus they will rejoice over the good of another as over their own good. Given this, insofar as the joy and felicity of anyone is increased, so the joy of all is increased: "Like all those rejoicing, [our dwelling is in you]" and so forth (Ps. [86:7]).

Hoc ergo habebunt illi qui erunt in uita eterna.

Mali autem, qui sunt in morte eterna, non minus habebunt de dolore et pena quam boni de gaudio et gloria. Exaggeratur uero pena eorum, primo ex separatione Dei et omnium bonorum; et est pena dampni, que maior est quam pena sensus: Matth. "Inutilem seruum eicite" etc. In uita enim ista mali habent tenebras interiores, scilicet peccata; sed tunc habebunt tenebras exteriores.

Secundo, ex remorsu conscientie: Ps. "Arguam te et statuam te"; Sap. Erunt "pre angustia spiritus gementes" etc. Tamen hec penitentia erit inutilis, quia non est propter odium malorum, sed propter timorem pene.

Tertio, ex immensitate pene sensibilis, scilicet ignis inferni qui animam et corpus cruciabit, et est acerbissima penarum, sicut sancti dicunt: nam erunt sicut semper morientes et nunquam mortui, unde etiam dicitur et mors eterna. Ps. "Mors depascet eos".

Quarto, ex desperatione. Nam si eis daretur spes liberationis a penis, eorum pena mitigaretur; sed quando subtrahitur eis omnis spes, tunc pena efficitur grauissima. Ysa. "Vermis eorum" etc.

Sic ergo apparet differentia inter bene operari et male, quia bona opera ducunt ad uitam, mala uero trahunt ad mortem; et propter hoc homines debent frequenter reducere ad memoriam, quia ex hoc prouocarentur ad bonum et retraherentur a malo. Vnde et signanter in fine omnium ponitur 'uita eterna', ut semper et magis memorie imprimatur.

In summa uero sciendum est quod secundum quosdam duodecim sunt articuli: sex de diuinitate, scilicet quod est unus Deus in essentia, et ideo dicitur 'Credo in unum Deum'; trinus in personis, et ideo dicitur 'Patrem et Filium et Spiritum Sanctum'; quod creator omnium, et ideo dicitur 'creatorem celi et terre'; quod ab eo sit omnis

Those who will be in eternal life will have all this. The wicked, however, who are in eternal death, will have no less sorrow or pain than the blessed have joy and glory. (2.1) Their pain will be exaggerated, first of all by separation from God and all good things. And this is the pain of loss, which is greater than the pain of the senses: "Cast the useless servant outside [into outer darkness; there one will weep and gnash one's teeth]" and so forth (Mt. [25:30]). In this life the wicked have interior darkness, that is to say, sinfulness, but then [in eternal death] they will have exterior darkness.

(2.2) [Their pain will be exaggerated] from remorse of conscience: "[You have done these things and I have been silent. You estimated wickedly that I was like you.] I will confront you and I will lay a charge [against you]" (Ps. [49:21]). And, "[Speaking among themselves in repentance, and] groaning in the stress of their spirit" and so forth (Wis. [5:3]). Nevertheless, this penitence will be useless, for it is not on account of hatred of evil, but of fear of pain.

(2.3) [Their pain will be exaggerated] from the immensity of pain that is of the senses, that is to say, of the fire of hell which is excruciating to soul and body, and which is the most bitter of pains (as the blessed saints do say). Indeed, they will be always dying but never dead, and this hell is called eternal death: "[Like sheep are put in the underworld,] death will pasture them" (Ps. [48:15]).

(2.4) [Their pain will be exaggerated] from despair, for if hope of freedom from pain were to be given to them, their pain would be mitigated. When all hope is withdrawn from them, however, then the pain is rendered most intense. And "[And they will go forth and look upon the body of those men who plotted against me;] their worm [will not die, and their fire will not be extinguished; and they will be so unto the satiation of the sight of all flesh]" and so forth (Is. [66:24]).

Therefore, the difference between living a good life and an evil life is clear, for good works lead up to life, but evil works draw down to death. For this reason humanity ought frequently to recollect itself, because from this [recollection] it will be spurred on to good and drawn back from evil. Thus, at the end of all [of the articles of the creed] eternal life is placed conspicuously, so that it may be impressed in memory always and ever more.

In summary, we should know that according to some [commentators] there are twelve articles [in the Apostles' Creed]; six about the divinity, that is to say, that there is essentially one God. Thus we say (1) "I believe in one God"; (2) three in persons, and thus we say "Father and Son and Holy Spirit"; (3) creator of all things, and thus we say "creator of heaven and earth"; (4) from God is all grace and the

gratia et remissio peccatorum; quod resuscitabit corpora nostra, et quod dabit bonis uitam eternam.

De humanitate autem sex similiter: scilicet quod conceptus et natus, quod mortuus et passus, quod descendit ad inferos, quod resurrexit tertia die, quod ascendit in celum, quod uenturus est ad iudicium etc.

Rogemus Dominum etc.

forgiveness of sins [the church, the communion of saints and the forgiveness of sins]; (5) God will raise up our bodies, and (6) God will give to the blessed eternal life.

Similarly, there are six [articles of the creed] about the humanity [of Christ]: namely, (1) conceived and born, (2) suffered and died, (3) descended into hell, (4) rose on the third day, (5) ascended into heaven, and (6) will come again to judge, and so forth.

Let us pray to the Lord, and so forth.

NOTES TO THE LATIN

Some manuscripts and the former printed versions of the Aquinas text add the following italicized text. For a fuller account see the forthcoming Leonine large-volume edition with the full and elaborate manuscript apparatus.

    1. sequere eum *qui est rex regum et dominus dominantium*

    2. potauerunt me aceto *augustinus super illud hebre. Qui proposito sibi gaudio sustinuit. Omnia bona terrena contempsit homo christus ihesus ut contempnenda monstraret*

    3. mundati erant per circumcisionem *uel ante circumcisionem qui saluati erant in fide parentum fidelium quantum ad eos qui non habebant usum rationis. uel per sacrificium et in fide christi venturi quantum ad adultos*

    4. frequenter debemus *solliciti esse illuc (descendere considerando penas) illas. sicut faciebat ille sanctus ezechias dicens*

    5. amico qui est in purgatorio *cum nulla sit comparatio penarum mundi ad illas.*

    6. differtur usque ad finem mundi, *nisi aliquibus ex priuilegio concedatur ut beate uirgini. et ut pie creditur beato iohanni euangeliste*

    7. partem omnium bonorum que fiunt in Ecclesia *et multa mala incurris ex perseuerancia in peccato. dyabolus etiam quanto diutius possidet tanto difficilius dimittit, ut dicit beda*

    8. penam inflictam peccatoribus *scilicet pena eterna O [rigenes] quam anguste erunt uie peccatoribus in iudicio. desuper erit iudex iratus etc.*

    9. "uniuersa delicta operit" *scilicet amor dei et proximi. que quidem caritas operit multitudinem peccatorum ut Ia. [petri] dicit*

    10. "Intra in gaudium Domini tui" *Augustinus. totum gaudium domini tui non intrabit in gaudentes sed toti gaudentes intrabunt in gaudium*

NOTES TO THE ENGLISH TRANSLATION

1. In the time of Aquinas there was no standard edition of the Vulgate, and manuscripts varied. Thomas generally used a recension known as the Parisian text, the one found in the critical edition of the Benedictines of San Girolamo, in the apparatus signed with the Greek Omega. Aquinas may have used many biblical manuscripts as he traveled about. Often he quoted from memory, or from liturgical usage, which may not have employed an exact quotation from Scripture. All the biblical translations from the Latin Vulgate are my own. They were made from the Clementine edition, with emendations in the edition of Sixtus V [Paris: Garnier Bros, 1868]. The Clementine edition was prepared by Clement VIII at the direction of the Council of Trent as a critical text for a printed version of the Vulgate. I chose that edition because it should be readily accessible to an inquiring reader. Since the quotations from Scripture in the "Collationes" are usually abbreviated, I often expand the biblical text in square brackets. Differences between the Aquinas scriptural text and the Vulgate text that I use are pointed out in the notes.

2. In the context of indefinite pronouns, the National Council of Teachers of English in their *Guidelines for Nonsexist Use of Language in NCTE Publications* claims: "In all but strictly formal usage, plural pronouns have become acceptable substitutes for the masculine singular." See the last part of the Introduction, which explains the various editorial strategies used to achieve sex-inclusive language.

3. Augustine may be commenting upon Romans 14:23. "Everything that is not of faith is sin."

4. Aquinas does not seem to quote John here in any precise way. He refers to his theology. Previous translations have pointed to John 17:3 as the particular source, but 1 John 3:2 might be even more helpful.

5. Aquinas cites Habakkuk, but actually quotes Hebrews 10:38, which itself refers back to Habakkuk.

6. This phrase does not seem to be an exact quote from Psalm 93. Perhaps it is a comment upon verse 11: "Dominus scit cogitationes hominum, quoniam vanae sunt" (The Lord knows the thoughts of humankind, and how they are vain).

7. The Vulgate text seems to be quoted inexactly here.

8. The quote from Isaiah in the Vulgate reads: "exaltabo solium meum." In Aquinas the quote reads: "ponam sedem meam." The previous English translators indicate Isaiah 14 as the source. Perhaps Aquinas quoted from memory,

or used a different biblical text. Scribal error is possible, or the reference to Isaiah may be in error.

9. Although I cannot find this exact quotation, previous English translators indicate Psalm 115:5, which does supply the correct context.

10. The reference to Augustine has not been identified.

11. The reference to Rabbi Moses has not been identified. Moses Maimonides may well be the source.

12. Chronicles in most contemporary bibles.

13. Photinus: fourth century disciple of Marcellus of Ancyra and bishop of Sirmium in Pannonia. He did not believe the Word of God was God, nor that Jesus Christ was more than a miraculous human being. Something of both Arius and Sabellius (see below) can be found in his position. Information taken from *A Catholic Dictionary*, 17th ed., ed. William Addis and Thomas Arnold (London: Routledge and Kegan Paul, 1960).

14. Sabellius (fl. c. 220): A doctrine proposed by him has been called monarchianism or modalism. It so insists upon the unity of the Divine Being that the Son has no reality separate from the Father. *New Catholic Encyclopedia* (New York: McGraw-Hill, 1967) 12:783. Hereinafter cited as *NCE*.

15. Arius (d. 336): Arianism denies the divinity of Christ and, subsequently, of the Holy Spirit. "Arius reduced the Christian Trinity to a descending triad, of whom the Father alone is true God." *NCE* 1:791.

16. *Consubstantialis* (*homoousion* in Greek) has been variously translated as "consubstantial," "of one substance," "of one essence," or "one in being." I prefer "one in being."

17. Aquinas here contrasts accident and substance.

18. This quotation comes from the "Fourth Responsory: Office of the Circumcision," in the *Dominican Breviary*.

19. Origen: "dixit quod Christus ad hoc natus est et venit in mundum saluaret etiam demones." This text would seem to be an indirect quotation, and it remains unidentified.

20. Manichaeus (b. 216): Manichaeism is a "complex dualistic religion essentially gnostic in character" (*NCE* 9:153).

21. Ebion: the Ebionites were a Jewish Christian sect that developed in the early Christian centuries. "Despite patristic mention of an Ebion as founder, the word actually refers to the 'poor men' (*ebjonim*) of the Beatitude (Mt. 5:3; Lk 4:18; 7:22)." Jesus was messiah because of his "eminent virtue achieved under the guidance of the Spirit received in the baptism of John whereby he kept the Law perfectly (i.e., was a saddiq)" (*NCE* 5:29).

22. Valentinus: a Gnostic leader, founder of a widespread sect in Rome in the second century. "Christ united with the man, Jesus, who was conceived of in a purely Docetic sense, to effect the conquest of death and the salvation of mankind" (*NCE* 14:518-19). Thus, the divinity in Jesus made only an appearance in the flesh.

23. Apollinaris of Laodicea (d. c. 390): He disputed whether "Christ had

a soul, thinking that His divine personality supplied the assumed human nature with that function" (NCE 1:668). This doctrine would undermine the full humanity of Christ.

24. Eutyches (d. 454): Constantinopolitan abbot, considered the father of monophysitism, which proposed that the human nature of Christ was absorbed into the divinity by the incarnation. *NCE* 5:642.

25. Nestorius (d. 451): Patriarch of Constantinople. He proposed that Mary was mother of Christ (*christotokos*) but not properly the mother of God (*theotokos*). *NCE* 10:348. This doctrine threatens the one person of Christ, both fully human and fully divine.

26. The "Declaration on the Relationship of the Church to Non-Christian Religions" (*Nostra Aetate*), issued as a document of Vatican II, would protect the human dignity of the members of all religions. In particular, the death of Christ is not to be blamed on "all Jews then living without distinction, nor upon the Jews of today." Anti-Semitism is repudiated "at any time and from any source."

27. Gregory the Great: "nihil nasci profuit nisi redimi profuisset." Taken from the "Exsultet" song of the *Praeconium Paschale* during the Holy Saturday liturgy at the solemn blessing of the Paschal candle. It is likely that the text was attributed to Gregory without foundation.

28. The Leonine edition indicates this quotation is from Baruch. The editions of Vivès and of Parma, however, locate the quotation in Acts, as indicated above, and they also give the quotation that Acts took from Habakkuk: "A work done in your days, which no one will believe when it is told" (1:5).

29. Aquinas would seem to betray here a common prejudice held in the Middle Ages against the Jews for the death of Christ.

30. Aquinas's quotation slightly rearranges some of the words of these parallel clauses.

31. After this last sentence, the Leonine edition does not reproduce some twenty words of text found in the Vivès and the Parma editions.

32. Augustine: "passio Christi sufficit ad informandum totaliter vitam nostram." The Latin text does not indicate this is an exact quotation. The reference has not been identified.

33. The quotation from Colossians was not noticed in the Vivès or the Parma editions, nor their English translations.

34. The commentary on this article ends with a quotation from Augustine in the Parma edition, but not in the Vivès nor in the Leonine.

35. I refer to the devil with the masculine pronoun, partly because the Latin is diabolus, and partly because the narratives in the Bible, in Dante, and in Milton refer to the devil as masculine.

36. Augustine: "per missas, per eleemoynas et per orationes." The Latin text does not indicate this is an exact quotation. The reference has not been identified.

37. Gregory: "addit quartum, scilicet per jejunium." The Latin text does not indicate this is an exact quotation. The reference has not been identified.

38. Although the Leonine gives Romans 8 (perhaps 8:34) as the source of this quotation, it would appear to be Acts.

39. Text here in the Vivès edition, which describes the effects of sin and remaining in the sway of the devil, is not included in the Leonine.

40. Aquinas does not quote Isaiah exactly.

41. Aquinas does not quote Hebrews here in an exact way.

42. The Leonine text reads: "Where *your eye* is." The eye, of course, is the window of the soul, and the desire of the eyes might have been an equivalent of "where your treasure is. . . ."

43. *Regula fidei*, or rule of faith, meant the normative and authoritative teaching of the church on the essential doctrine of faith. Here it is synonymous with the creed.

44. Gregory: "differentia inter judicandos: quia judicandi aut sunt boni, aut sunt mali." The Latin text does not indicate this is an exact quotation. The reference has not been identified.

45. The Wisdom text actually reads: "there will be questioning into the thoughts of the wicked."

46. The quotation from I Peter is not exact.

47. "De Trinitate" IX,10: "Verbum est igitur, quod nunc discernere ac insinuare volumus, cum amore notitia." *PL* 42:969. The Leonine edition direct quotation reads: "Verbum quod insinuare intendimus cum amore notitia est."

48. Priscilla and Montanus: second-century illuminati who claimed special charismatic gifts of the Spirit. *NCE* 9:1078.

49. God also created everything through Christ. In the Trinity, the external work attributed to one Person is the work of all three Persons in reality.

50. "De Divinis Nominibus," chapter IV, section 11. The Latin gives a direct quotation. See "On Divine Names" in *The Works of Dionyius the Areopagite*, trans. John Parker (Merrick, N.Y.: Richwood Pub. Co., 1976), p. 45.

51. After the quote from Proverbs, the Mandonnet text adds two very similar and reenforcing quotations: (1) the woman who washed the feet of Jesus with her tears and was told "her many sins are forgiven because she loved much" (Luke 7:47), and (2) "Charity covers a multitude of sins" (1 Pet. 4:8).

52. Ecclesiasticus 51:31 is not found in all contemporary bibles, but it is found in the Latin Vulgate.

53. The quotation from Ephesians 4:4 is not exact in the Aquinas text.

54. The John 17:22 quotation speaks of the Father and the Son being one, and the prayer of Jesus asks that his followers likewise be one.

55. See Apocalypse 1:5. Jesus "who loved us, and washed us from our sins in his own blood."

56. Chrism oil is used in the dedication of a church.

57. The quotations from 2 Corinthians 1:21 and from 1 Corinthians 6:11 only loosely follow the Vulgate text, which text I give in translation.

58. Donatists: fourth-century Christian sect who are often characterized by an "exaggerated insistence on the holiness of the minister in the confection of Sacramental rites" (*NCE* 4:1001).

59. The word, "peter," is related to the word for "rock." See Matthew 16:18. "You are Peter and upon this rock I will build my church. . . ."

60. The Aquinas text differs here from the Vulgate.

61. The Maccabees quotation has not been found. Perhaps 2 Maccabees 7:18. See also 1 Thessalonians 4:12: "We do not wish you to be ignorant, brothers, of those who fall asleep, so that you be not saddened as are the rest of people who have no hope."

62. The Latin for this passage about time and eternity is not clear.

63. The Sadducees did not hold a doctrine of the resurrection of the body, which they could not find in the Torah. The Pharisees, however, did have a hope of resurrection, based on later writings in the Scriptures.

64. This quotation only approximates the Vulgate. The reference may be wrong. The Latin indicates only Exodus. Genesis 15:1 should also be considered.

65. Augustine: "Videbimus, et amabimus, et laudabimus," etc., *City of God*, Bk. XXII, 30. These are almost the last words of the book. The Latin text gives a direct quotation.

66. Augustine: "Fecisti nos, Domine, ad te," etc., *Confessions*, I, 1. The Latin text gives a direct quotation.

DIVISIONS OF THE APOSTLES' CREED

The rudiments of a creed can be found in the sacred scriptures of any religion. Creeds make explicit what may appear in the sacred text implicitly. Creeds distill the essentials, whereas commentaries more leisurely elaborate and illustrate matters. Thomas Aquinas says in the *Summa Theologica* that "the articles of faith stand in the same relation to the doctrine of faith as self-evident principles to a teaching based on natural reason" (II, 2, Q1, A7). Ambrose reminds the catechumens about to be baptized that the creed is a breviary of faith: "The holy apostles, gathered together as one, composed a breviary of faith, so that we might comprehend briefly the scope of our entire faith."[1]

Beginnings of the creed antedate the writing of the Gospels and Letters of the New Testament. Elements of the creed are among the most ancient formulations of Christian belief that we know of. Just as the Christian community told the stories of Jesus and their understanding of him in oral tradition long before the Gospels and Letters of Paul were written, so the community formulated a rite of baptism and a way of introducing Christians to the content of belief long before there was anything like a fixed creed. Even in Rome, the church wrote largely in Greek during the first century, and fragments of these Greek writings with roots in the apostolic age and later texts in Latin provide a fairly reliable reconstruction of the Old Roman Creed. This creed of the church of Rome both borrowed from and lent to many other creedal formulations of doctrine. In particular, it would seem to be the ancestral foundation of all Western baptismal creeds. The Old Roman Creed, sometimes called the *Romanum*, gives the pithy substance of the established text (*textus receptus*) of the Apostles' Creed as we know it today.

The work of reconstructing the Apostles' Creed from the contribution of many creeds local to many churches in various times and places has left a trail of scholarly investigation.[2] Often the conclusions about the historical genesis of the creed remain provisional. Given what we know today, such a tentative explanation seems most plausible. The crystallization of tradition resists the consistency and clarity of a logical outline. Marcellus of Ancyra in Asia Minor wrote in Greek a letter (c. 341) to Pope Julius I which repeated what is now thought to be the Old Roman Creed as the creed Marcellus himself in fact espoused.[3] Rufinus of Aquileia, who wrote a theological com-

mentary on the creed of Aquileia (c. 400), gives some indirect information about the *Romanum*.[4] He mentions in detail how the creed of Rome differed from that of Aquileia. For example, in his comments about the "descent into hell," he mentions that this clause was not found in the *Romanum*.

The established text is more fulsome than the Old Roman Creed. There are several late additions. Their inclusion in what became the established text dates between the fourth and eighth centuries, even though the doctrines were themselves much older. Their introduction to the creed was gradual, with some instances earlier than others. Nicetas of Remesiana gives us almost the established text of the Apostles' Creed[5] (c. 400), but the first example of the text of the Apostles' Creed in exactly the version we know it today (*textus receptus*) would seem to come from St. Priminius[6] (c. 725).

Manuscripts of the creeds did not usually break the articles of faith into numbered articles. Most manuscripts run the sentences one after the other in a tight economical order to conserve parchment. Not only were numbers not found, but punctuation that might have indicated where one article of the creed stopped and the next one began is often very spare. Moreover, the pious tradition of not writing the creed down, but of inscribing it in one's heart, led to a certain paucity of written copies. Christians were to memorize the creed, to meditate upon it in their prayer, and to live it in their life as a disciple of Christ, rather than write it down somewhere and then proceed to forget all about it. Many of the instructions given to catechumens at the time of their baptism make much of this Christian practice of rendering the creed by memory.[7] Instructions in the faith were given personally and orally to the catechumen by the local church into which he or she was to be incorporated by baptism. Local liturgies and local creeds were various and the text often in flux.

Despite the idiosyncrasy of so much of liturgical practice and creedal formulation, it is surprising how many creeds agree upon the basic outline of the doctrine of faith. Clearly the creeds followed the "rule of faith" and a genuine and ancient apostolic tradition, and that was their least common denominator. Nonetheless, the question before us now as students of the Apostles' Creed remains this. How shall we articulate the creed? What are the articles of faith? If we do a study of the comparative anatomy of the body of the creed, where are the joints? Which bones belong in what classification? The creed remains an organic body of truths that are interrelated like the members of a body, and yet the tibia is not the fibula. How many articles of faith are there and what are their proper names?

The threefold division of the creed, corresponding to the three declarations of faith in the Father, the Son, and the Holy Spirit, does establish an overall trinitarian pattern. The creed divides into three sections, each a "credo in" statement directed to each person of the Trinity. Following the dominical command in Matthew, early baptismal rites were generally a threefold question: Do you believe in the Father? Do you believe in Jesus Christ, his only Son? Do you believe in the Holy Spirit? The declarative creeds grew out of the interrogatory creed as a natural amplification of the text to accommodate the need for teaching and preaching, and a desired expansion of doctrine.

Nevertheless, tradition would hold there are twelve articles in the Apostles' Creed. The popular legend has long claimed that the Apostles' Creed represents in some way the twelve apostles and their teaching. Rufinus of Aquileia notes the tradition (or more exactly, the legend) that each of the apostles contributed one article of the creed. According to his commentary, after the descent of the Holy Spirit at Pentecost and prior to the dispersal of the apostles throughout the world to preach the risen Christ, they composed together a formulation of their faith. Each of them was invited to contribute one article to affirm in unity and consensus the essence of their belief in Jesus of Nazareth.

Rufinus does not assign each article of the creed to a particular apostolic author. Priminius, however, who gives us the established text several centuries later, does attribute each of the articles of the creed to a particular apostle as author. His listing does not completely agree in attribution with other authors, such as Pseudo-Augustine, who give a somewhat different account. Nevertheless, when biographical lists are compared, the order of the names of the apostles remains more or less consistent and seems to conform roughly to the order of being chosen apostles by Jesus himself as recounted in the synoptic Gospels, where agreement is also more or less consistent.

The legend of the apostolic authorship of the Apostles' Creed has ancient roots. Both Henri deLubac and J. N. D. Kelly believe that Ambrose of Milan in a letter to Pope Siricius in Rome (c. 390) gives the first clear reference to generic apostolic authorship.[8] Rufinus gives the first undisputed reference to the Apostles' Creed as the work of the twelve apostles as authors, and furthermore he claims specific authorship, while not giving a list attributing each article to one specific apostle. Depending on how you date his writing (? sixth to eighth century), Pseudo-Augustine may be the first claimant to a listing of articles composed by specific apostles. Pseudo-Augustine, however

gives us two differing lists of specific authorship. Sermon 240 follows the order in the *Missale Romanum*, where the eucharistic canon's listing of the apostles is of ancient origin. Sermon 241[9] follows Acts (1:13). Priminius (c. 725) gives a list of specific authorship that follows Acts, and may also be found in the creed in the Gallican Sacramentary (c. 650). See the chart and chart notes below.

In the medieval period, details about this specific authorship were elaborated. Bonaventure's *Breviloquium*[10] elaborates corresponding Old Testament figures in sets of twelve. Alcuin[11] has a listing of specific authorship that follows the order of the twelve apostles in Matthew (10:2–4). Alexander of Hales,[12] Thomas Aquinas, and others investigated this question of the division of the articles of faith and their specific authorship. The coming of the Renaissance period saw the culmination of the legend in its depiction in liturgical representations, and in particular paintings and carvings in many churches of France and Germany in the fifteenth century. At the same time, the awakening of a critical revisioning began the discrediting of the legend in so much of its particularity. The Greek representatives to the Council of Florence (1438–45) argued cogently that they knew of no Apostles' Creed with apostolic authorship, either generic or specific. If there had been such a text, written by the apostles in some collaborative way, there would have been a record of it surely in the Acts of the Apostles. Legends, however, do not disappear immediately, and even as late as the sixteenth century, long after the legend of apostolic authorship was in decline, the Council of Trent continued to number twelve articles to the creed, although without specific attribution to any of the twelve apostles.

The usual order of attribution is as follows. Peter is always given Article One, "I believe in God." Matthias, who took Judas's place and was last chosen, is almost always given Article Twelve. James and John, the close associates of Jesus, who are brothers and the sons of Zebedee, usually are given Articles Two and Three. Then Andrew, brother of Simon Peter, is given Article Four. This order follows Mark (3:16–19) and Acts (1:13). In all the synoptic Gospels it is Philip who is next chosen, and usually he is given the next article, which is usually reckoned to be the "descent into hell." On all lists I have seen Thomas is given the next article, dealing with the resurrection, even though such an attribution puts him out of the order of apostolic selection in all the Gospels, although not in Acts nor in the eucharistic canon of the *Missale Romanum*. No doubt John's account of the "doubting Thomas" made it irresistible to attribute the resurrection article of faith to Thomas the Apostle. The Gospels list the order of selection

after Philip to be: Bartholomew, and then Matthew and Thomas, (vice versa in Matthew), then James the lesser (son of Alphaeus). Finally, Thaddeus (Jude or Judas, not Iscariot) is followed by Simon the Zealot (vice versa in Luke), with Judas Iscariot always listed as the last. The attribution to the articles of the creed follows roughly this order: Peter, James and John, and Andrew always head the list, though Andrew is sometimes second, following Matthew (10:2–4) and Luke (6:14–16) and the *Missale Romanum*. Philip is given the "descent into hell"; Thomas is given the resurrection article. Simon, Jude, and Matthias can be counted on at the end of the list. The remainder fill in, now this way, now that.

Ancient legends are often discredited by the simple declaration that no historical evidence to support the legend can be found. At the same time, there is usually no evidence to disprove the legend either. There is simply no reliable evidence about it one way or the other. No one today believes in the specific authorship of the Apostles' Creed by each apostle contributing a particular article. Nor is it likely that a generic authorship of the Apostles' Creed by the apostles in some collegial way, and even over some period of time, can be maintained. And yet the apostolic authorship of the creed is not in question, if authorship is understood as the authority behind the text, regardless of who edited and redacted the exact words. In that same vein, we have the authentic teaching of Jesus, but very little if any of his *ipsissima verba*. With the Apostles' Creed we have the teaching of the apostles as passed on by an authentic apostolic succession. The meanderings and complex history of the exact wording may not ever be discovered. The authority of the Gospels has no greater apostolic authenticity, for it too represents the community rendering of the teaching of the apostles more than the direct apostolic authoring of the Gospels themselves. The creed summarizes the Scriptures, which in turn summarize the teaching of the early church by the apostles, who in turn were taught of Jesus, who was taught of God.

While the legend of the apostolic authorship has not held up, the apostolic authority of the creed does still deserve our allegiance. This text is an ancient and authentic one, distilled over centuries by many communities of faith, and jealously and carefully guarded as the substance of belief to be taught catechumens, who deserved pure and simple Christian doctrine. Although legends are rarely shown to be historical, legends tell us what the people who constructed them wanted from their creed and its origin. They desired a text that was derived from Jesus, through his close associates and apostles, who knew his words. They wished a doctrine that had not been corrupted

by the passage of time or by changes of wording. In short, in this legend of the apostolic authorship, the faithful wanted a pure, ample, unadulterated, and perduring revealed truth about God and his loving ways for human beings. If one must disown the direct authorship of the apostles, one need not disown the guidance of the Holy Spirit that led the church through its historical vicissitudes to craft and protect this ancient formulation of the essence of the faith precisely embodied with an ancient and sacred authority in the Apostles' Creed of the West and the Niceno-Constantinopolitan Creed of the East.

Given the legend of the twelve apostles composing the creed article by article, and given the tradition of twelve articles that survives to this day, the question should now be raised how shall we compose these articles? There has not been unanimity about the divisions of the Apostles' Creed. I find there are twenty clauses in the Apostles' Creed. These are as follows:

1. I believe in God
2. Father almighty
3. Creator of heaven and earth
4. And in Jesus Christ
5. His only Son our Lord
6. Conceived by the Holy Spirit
7. Born of the virgin Mary
8. Suffered under Pontius Pilate, was crucified
9. Was dead, was buried.
10. Descended into hell
11. On the third day he rose again
12. He ascended into heaven
13. Sits at the right hand of God the Father
14. He will come to judge the living and the dead
15. I believe in the Holy Spirit
16. The holy catholic church
17. The communion of saints
18. The forgiveness of sins
19. The resurrection of the body
20. (And) life everlasting.

These twenty clauses must be reduced to twelve articles, if the tradition is to be maintained. Eight clauses must be yoked. Almost everyone agrees that 1 and 2 and 3 should go together, and that the pairing of 4 and 5, 6 and 7, and 8 and 9 seems reasonable. There is hardly an example that does not yoke 12 and 13. Thus only two more

clauses must be combined. No one puts forth "the communion of saints," which is a late established addition, to stand alone as a separate article. However, there remains endless controversy over whether it belongs with "holy church" or with "the forgiveness of sins."[13] The issue thus reduces itself to finding one more clause to yoke, and the candidates are either "the descent into hell" or "life everlasting." Both of these are not found in the Old Roman Creed, and as late established additions they have been moved about in the creed.

The problem could be solved in one of two ways: (1) the "descent into hell" is yoked, either by joining it with "suffered, was crucified, was dead, and was buried, *and descended into hell*," or by combining it with the following article. Thus "*he descended into hell*; the third day he rose again from the dead." (2) The other possibility is to yoke "life everlasting" with "the resurrection of the body." That has been done in many creeds, and the frequent presence of the conjunction "and" lends some argument to so doing. Thus, "the resurrection of the body and life everlasting" would become the last article of the creed. If the "descent" is yoked, then the "resurrection of the body" remains the eleventh article of the creed, and "life everlasting" the twelfth. The chart gives a picture of the complexity of this matter.

Thomas Aquinas divided the articles of faith into twelve in his "De Articulis Fidei,"[14] even though these twelve do not follow the traditional division. He talks about the enumeration of the articles of the creed in two places: (1) the *Summa Theologica*, II, 2, Q1, A.8, "Whether the Articles of Faith are suitably enumerated?" and (2) in the *Compendium Theologiae*, Caput 246, "Of the Distinction of the Articles of Faith." His divisions are most logical, even though they depart considerably from the traditional division of the articles of faith in the many examples of the creed in the early centuries. Thomas's divisions primarily serve the purposes of the systematic theologian, rather than the conservation of the older tradition.

Aquinas's twelvefold division divides the articles evenly in two parts: six articles appertain to the divinity of God, and six to the humanity of Jesus Christ. Let us give the six articles that treat the divinity: (1) "I believe in God" addresses the unity of God; (2) "the Father Almighty" includes the Son and the Spirit by implication within the mystery of the Trinity; (3) "creator of heaven and earth" addresses the whole creation of the world; (4) "holy, catholic church; communion of saints, and forgiveness of sins" are run together to speak of the present work of grace and sanctification in the world; and finally (5) "resurrection of the body" and (6) "life everlasting" as separate articles concern themselves with the glory to come in the parousia. Let us

give the six articles that treat the humanity: (1) "conceived by the spirit and born of the virgin Mary"; (2) "suffered . . . buried"; (3) "descent into hell"; (4) "rose again"; (5) "ascended into heaven . . ." and (6) "from thence he will come to judge the living and the dead."

Aquinas's fourteenfold division also divides the articles evenly in two parts: seven articles appertain to the divinity of God, and seven to the humanity of Jesus Christ. Let us give the seven articles that treat the divinity: (1) "I believe in God" addresses the unity of God. (2) "The Father Almighty," (3) "Jesus Christ his only Son Our Lord," and (4) "I believe in the Holy Spirit" concern themselves with the three persons of the Trinity. (5) "Creator of heaven and earth" addresses the creation of the world; (6) "holy, catholic church; communion of saints, and forgiveness of sins" elaborate the work of grace and sanctification; and (7) "resurrection of the body and life everlasting" combined in one article speaks of the glory to come in the parousia. Let us give the seven articles that treat the humanity: (1) "conceived by the Holy Spirit" becomes a separate article, followed by (2) "born of the virgin Mary." The remaining five articles follow the traditional narration of the deeds of Christ: (3) "suffered," (4) "descent into hell," (5) "rose again," (6) "ascended into heaven," (7) "will come to judge."

In his "Collationes Credo in Deum,"[15] Aquinas uses a yet different fourteenfold division of the articles of faith. Chapters here each represent a sermon-conference or "collatio" preached in the vernacular during the last Lenten season of Thomas's life (1273) in the parish church of Naples. Two sermons are devoted to the first article of faith: "I believe in one God." Aquinas then runs through the Apostles' Creed article by article in much the same way as Priminius. The "descent into hell" is given separate article status, and so are "the resurrection of the body" and "life everlasting." The "communion of saints" is yoked with "the forgiveness of sins." The extra "collation" devoted to "I believe in God" adds another number to the traditional twelve, and the separate status of the "descent" as well as "the resurrection of the body" and "life everlasting" adds in effect another clause to make up the fourteen. The chart that follows this chapter illustrates these divisions.

In the *Summa Theologica*, Thomas divides theology into three parts. The first (Prima Pars) discusses the divinity of God bestowing itself upon the world "and of those things which came forth from the power of God in accordance with his will." In the second part (Secunda Pars, I et II) Aquinas discusses the image of God which is man "according as he too is the principle of his actions, as having free choice and control of his actions." In the third part (Tertia Pars) Thomas

treats of Christ, "the Saviour of all, and of the benefits bestowed by him on the human race." In Aquinas's twelvefold and fourteenfold divisions of the creed, he follows this same scheme of the *Summa*.[16] The first half of the articles (either six or seven of them) deals with the divinity of God just as the Prima Pars; the second half of the creed deals with the humanity of Christ, just as the Tertia Pars. The Secunda Pars of the *Summa* is absent from the creed, which does not treat explicitly the rational and moral behavior of humanity in its return to God. Only by implication from what is said about God will one find a blueprint for human behavior in the creed, which gives rather the deeds of God: Father, Son and Holy Spirit.

My own solution to the articulation of the creed follows Priminius primarily. I offer my own arguments for this arrangement, lacking any from Priminius. The "communion of saints" is yoked with "forgiveness of sins." The controversy is extensive, and the only argument I want to put forth here is that there is a parallel with the Niceno-Constantinopolitan Creed's formulation: "one baptism for the forgiveness of sins." Thus the sacraments of the church are put together and given emphasis. Furthermore, "resurrection of the body" is yoked with "and life everlasting." Both phrases are given in the Nicene Creed, and they are found together with the conjunction. Moreover, "resurrection of the body" and "life everlasting" appear to be twin ideas, such as space and time. They are not the same thing, but they are related closely and easily combined in one article.

Along with Priminius and a few others I am arguing for making the "descent into hell" a separate article of the Apostles' Creed. If it is combined with "suffered . . . buried," which the numbering in Trent does, it sounds like the "descent" only means Jesus was truly dead and buried. Some contemporary translations, such as the International Commission on English in the Liturgy (ICEL), read that "he descended to the *dead*. If it is combined with "third day he rose again," as most contemporary commentators do, it steals the thunder of the resurrection article, and it appears to point only to that anticipation of resurrection that is found in the tradition of the harrowing of hell by the already risen Jesus. I should like the "descent" to keep both meanings and belong to both articles on either side of it. The simplest way to have it both ways would seem to be to place it as a separate article, sandwiched between the passion and the resurrection. The early commentators, who assign the twelve apostles by name, generally give the "descent" entirely to some one of them, customarily Philip or Thomas.

Aquinas in the idiosyncratic division of the articles of faith in his "De Articulis Fidei" still gives the "descent" separate status. In his "Expositio Super Symbolum" he also gives the "descent" separate status, although he there divides the Apostles' Creed into fourteen articles. Both of the previous English translations[17] rearrange the fourteenfold division of Aquinas to fit a twelvefold expectation, and they therefore combine the descent with the resurrection article to help make fourteen fit into twelve. An argument against giving the "descent" separate article status could possibly be made from its absence in the Eastern creeds. And yet, we find the doctrine of the "descent" well established in the Eastern fathers. The very influential catechetical instructions of Cyril of Jerusalem talk of the "descent" in several places.

The arrangement of the articles of faith does provide an immediate practical problem. How shall the material of a commentary be presented in chapter and divisions? But beyond that, does the division of the articles of the creed suggest different understandings of the given article? If the "descent into hell" is placed with the "passion" does it necessarily have a different meaning, or at least emphasis, compared to being yoked with the "resurrection" article? Does the "communion of saints" take on one meaning when joined with the "church" article, and another when combined with "forgiveness of sins"? In effect, does it refer to the people of God or the sacraments that they share? Furthermore, is "life eternal" more synonymous with "resurrection of the body" when these two are joined with the conjunction? These are fair questions.

Let us try to answer them. It could be that where an article is positioned already reflects how that article was understood. It could also be that where an article is placed contributed to how the article has become understood. In short, the positioning could be consequence or it could be cause. It is also possible that it makes no difference how it is placed, even if the positioning was once done deliberately. Texts are read often without adverting to format, that may even be a matter only of editorial thoughtlessness. This is my own view. We cannot show why the positioning happened as it did, and in fact, there is no one incontrovertible orthodox arrangement of the text. The Vatican standardized the text of the creed largely to facilitate prayer in common, but such a disciplinary decree does not pretend to be historical validation for the exact wording and composition of articles. The evidence for a historical solution of how exactly to divide the articles of faith remains indecisive, and what I put forth is an arrangement or articulation with pedagogic advantages and as much histori-

cal support as an opposite division. The chart that follows will give some of the data which might assist the reader to follow the argument and to make his or her own best conclusion. How the articles are set up in any commentary will accomplish this much. It will call attention to where the emphasis is being placed, and make one reading easier to support than another. I would claim little more than this.

Obviously, one need not keep the twelvefold division, which may seem a mere remnant of the legend of direct apostolic authorship. The tradition of twelve articles will seem to some commentators on the creed worth keeping in order to hold a continuity with the past. Nevertheless, were one to depart from the tradition, there would be many rational schemes for dividing the creed. As we have seen, Aquinas offers two such schemes for re-arranging the divisions of the creed. No doubt any student of the creed could propose other arrangements.

NOTES

1. "Explanatio Symboli ad Initiandos" in J. P. Migne, *Patrologiae Cursus Completus, Series Latina* (Paris, 1844–64), 17:1155. Hereinafter cited as *PL*.

2. J. N. D. Kelly, *Early Christian Creeds*, 3rd ed. (New York: David McKay Co., 1972). Hereinafter cited as *ECC*. If you can read only one book on the history of the creed, let me recommend this text.

3. Henricus Denzinger, *Enchiridion Symbolorum*, 32nd ed. (Rome: Herder, 1963) no. 11, p. 21. Hereinafter cited as Denzinger.

4. "Commentarius in Symbolum Apostolorum" *PL* 21:335–86. See also "A Commentary on the Apostles' Creed," in *Ancient Christian Writers*, vol. 20, trans. J. N. D. Kelly (Westminster, Md.: Newman, 1955). Kelly's introduction is very helpful in giving a succinct historical overview.

5. Denzinger, no. 19, p. 24.

6. "De Singulis Libris Canonicis Scarapsus," *PL* 89:1029. Priminius is sometimes written Pirminius.

7. For example, see Augustine, Sermon 212, *PL* 38:1058ff.

8. For further information about the legend of the twelve apostles, see J. N. D. Kelly's "The Ancient Legend" in *ECC*, pp. 1–6. Henri deLubac's "The History of a Legend" in *Christian Faith: The Structure of the Apostles' Creed* (San Francisco: Ignatius Press, 1986), pp. 19–55, gives a masterful summary of this fascinating story. Both of these books are mines of information about the Apostles' Creed. See also "The Gradual Formation of the Apostles' Creed," an elaborate historical chart done by Philip Schaff in his *The Creeds of Christendom*, vol. 2 (New York: Harper and Bros., 1877) pp. 52–55.

9. *PL* 39:2189–90.

10. *Breviloquium*, trans. Erwin E. Nemmers (London: B. Herder, 1946), V:7, "The Practice of Grace in Regard to What Is to Be Believed," pp. 163–64.

11. "Disputatio Puerorum," *PL* 101:1140.

12. *Summa Theologica,* Bk 3, Pt 3, Inq 2, Tract 2, Q 2, Titulus 1, "De Symbolo Apostolorum."

13. Stephen Benko, *The Meaning of Sanctorum Communio* (Chatham, Eng.: Mackay and Co., 1964). This book gives an exhaustive scholarly study of the various readings of the phrase "communion of saints." He concludes that "sanctorum communio" refers primarily to the sacraments (neuter *sanctorum*) and not to the membership of the church (masculine *sanctorum*).

14. "De Articulis Fidei" can be found in *Opuscula Theologica et Philosophica,* Parma (16:115); Vivès (27:171); Marietti (1:141).

15. "Collationes Credo in Deum" can be found under the title "Expositio Super Symbolum Apostolorum," Parma (16:97), Vivès (27:144), Mandonnet (4:349); and Marietti (2:191).

16. Taken from the preface to each part of the *Summa Theologica.*

17. *The Catechetical Instructions of St. Thomas Aquinas* trans. Joseph B. Collins (New York: Joseph Wagner, 1939). And *The Three Greatest Prayers,* trans. Laurence Shapcote, O.P. (Westminster, Md.: Newman, 1956).

Articles of the Creed[1]	I	II	III	IV	V
Mark 3:16–19[2]	Peter	James	John	Andrew	Philip
Matthew 10:2–4[2]	Peter	Andrew	James	John	Philip
Luke 6:14–16[2]	Peter	Andrew	James	John	Philip
Acts 1:13[2]	Peter	John	James	Andrew	Philip
Priminius[3]	Peter	John	James	Andrew	Philip
Gallican Sacramentary[4]	Peter	John	James	Andrew	Philip
Missale Romanum[5]	Peter	Andrew	James	John	Thomas
Pseudo-Augustine[6]	Peter	Andrew	James	John	Thomas
Priminius[3]	1,2,3	4,5	6,7	8,9	10
Gallican Sacramentary[4]	1,2,3	4,5	6,7	8,9	10
Pseudo-Augustine[6]	1,2,3	4,5	6,7	8,9	10,11
Aquinas Collationes[7]	1 (2)	2,3	4,5	6,7	8,9
Council of Trent[8]	1,2,3	4,5	6,7	8,9,10	11
Harmonia Symbolica[9]	1,2,3	4,5	6,7	8,9	10,11
Aquinas "De Articulis Fidei"[10]	1	2,4,5,15	3	16,17,18	19
Aquinas (14)[11]	1	2	4,5	15	3

1. The twelve articles of the creed might reasonably be divided into twenty clauses as follows:

    1. I believe in God
    2. Father almighty
    3. Creator of heaven and earth
    4. And in Jesus Christ
    5. His only Son our Lord
    6. Conceived by the Holy Spirit
    7. Born of the virgin Mary
    8. Suffered under Pontius Pilate, was crucified
    9. Was dead, was buried
    10. Descended into hell
    11. On the third day he rose again
    12. He ascended into heaven
    13. Sits at the right hand of God the Father
    14. He will come to judge the living and the dead
    15. I believe in the Holy Spirit
    16. The holy catholic church
    17. The communion of saints
    18. The forgiveness of sins
    19. The resurrection of the body
    20. (And) life everlasting

2. The apostles are listed in four places in the New Testament (Mark 3:16–19; Mt. 10:2–4; Luke 6:14–16, and Acts 1:13). Although there is general agreement about the order of names, there are no two lists exactly the same. The names of the apostles are: Peter (Simon called Peter), James (the greater, son of Zebedee and brother of John), John (son of Zebedee and brother of James the greater), Andrew (brother of Simon Peter), Philip, Bartholomew (probably the same person as Nathaniel in John 1:45 and 21:2), Thomas (also called Didymus, which means twin), Matthew (also called Levi), James

VI	VII	VIII	IX	X	XI	XII	XIII	XIV
Barth	Matthew	Thomas	James	Jude	Simon	Judas		
Barth	Thomas	Matthew	James	Jude	Simon	Judas		
Barth	Matthew	Thomas	James	Simon	Jude	Judas		
Thomas	Barth	Matthew	James	Simon	Jude	Matthias		
Thomas	Barth	Matthew	James	Simon	Jude	(2) Thomas		
Thomas	Barth	Matthew	James	Simon	Jude	Matthias		
James	Philip	Barth	Matthew	Simon	Jude			
James	Philip	Barth	Matthew	Simon	Jude	Matthias		
11	12, 13	14	15	16	17, 18	19, 20		
11	12, 13	14	15	16	17, 18	19, 20		
12, 13	14	15	16, 17	18	19	20		
10	11	12, 13	14	15	16	17, 18	19	20
12, 13	14	15	16, 17	18	19	20		
12, 13	14	15	16, 17	18	19	20		
20	6, 7	8, 9	10	11	12, 13	14		
16, 17, 18	19, 20	6	7	8, 9	10	11	12, 13	14

(the lesser, and son of Alphaeus), Thaddeus (also called Jude, and Judas not Iscariot), Simon (the Zealot), Judas (Iscariot), and Matthias (chosen to replace the deceased Judas Iscariot).

3. "De Singulis Libris Canonicis Scarapsus." *PL* 89:1034. Priminius was the founding abbot of the Benedictine monastery of Reichenau near Lake Constance in the first half of the eighth century. Priminius (sometimes called Pirminius) follows the order in Acts.

4. Gallican Sacramentary (c. 650). See Charles Heurtley, *Harmonia Symbolica: A Collection of Creeds* (Oxford: Oxford University Press, 1858), pp. 67–68. This text follows the order in Acts.

5. *Missale Romanum*. This Latin prayerbook was in wide and official use for many centuries in Roman Catholicism. See this ancient Eucharistic Canon. The order of the apostles therein is *sui generis*, although the first four (Peter, Andrew, James and John) follow the gospels of Matthew and Luke.

6. *PL* 39:2189–90. Pseudo-Augustine: Sermon 240, which follows the order in the *Missale Romanum*. Sermon 241, attributed to the same author, is yet different and follows the order in Acts. He is thought to be a preacher, probably from Gaul, and writing at least a century or more after Augustine.

7. The "Collationes Credo in Deum" can be found under the title of "Expositio Super Symbolum Apostolorum" in the Parma (16:97), in the Vivès (27:144), in the Mandonnet (4:349), and in the Marietti (2:191) editions.

8. Henricus Denzinger, *Enchiridion Symbolorum*, 32nd ed. (Rome: Herder, 1963), no. 30, p. 28.

9. Heurtley, op. cit., pp. 118–20.

10. Aquinas, "De Articulis Fidei," which can be found in his *Opuscula Theologica et Philosophica*, Parma (16:115); Vivès (27:171); Marietti (1:141). See note below.

11. *Summa Theologica*, II, 2, Q1, A8. See also Aquinas, "Of the Distinction of the Articles of Faith," *Compendium Theologiae*, Caput 246, Parma 16:76.

VERSIONS OF THE APOSTLES' CREED

APOSTLES' CREED

parentheses = late established additions

I believe ᴧ

1   Credo in Deum
    Patrem Omnipotentem
    (Creatorem coeli et terrae)

2   Et in Jesum Christum
    Filium ejus unicum
    Dominum nostrum

3   Qui (conceptus) est de Spiritu Sancto
    Natus ex Maria Virgine

4   (Passus) sub Pontio Pilato, crucifixus
    (Mortuos) et sepultus

5   (Descendit ad inferna) [not in Nicene]

6   Tertia die resurrexit a mortuis

7   Ascendit ad coelos
    Sedet ad dexteram (Dei) Patris (omnipotentis)

8   Inde venturus est
    Judicare vivos et mortuous

9   Credo in Spiritum Sanctum

10 Sanctam Ecclesiam (Catholicam)

11 (Sanctorum Communionem) [not in Nicene]
    Remissionem peccatorum

12 Carnis resurrectionem,
    (Et vitam aeternam).

This creed identifies the late established additions to the Apostles' Creed. The text is based on Charles Heurtley's *Harmonia Symbolica: A Collection of Creeds* (Oxford: Oxford University Press, 1858), pp. 118–20. I have arranged the articles of the creed, following the scheme explained in Appendix I. Thus, "the descent," "the communion of saints" and the "resurrection of the body" differ in their position from that of Heurtley. I also include the "et" before "vitam aeternam." Neither Heurtley nor Denzinger (no. 30), which gives the standardized text from the *Breviarium Romanum* include this conjunction. Along with J. N. D. Kelly, I take the "et" from the *Ordo Romanus Antiquus*.

189

ICET TRANSLATION

1. I believe in God, the Father almighty,
2.   creator of heaven and earth.
3. I believe in Jesus Christ, his only Son, our Lord.
4.   He was conceived by the power of the Holy Spirit
5.   and born of the Virgin Mary.
6. He suffered under Pontius Pilate,
7.   was crucified, died, and was buried.
8. He descended to the dead.
9. On the third day he rose again.
10. He ascended into heaven,
11.   and is seated at the right hand of the Father.
12. He will come again to judge the living and the dead.
13. I believe in the Holy Spirit,
14.   the holy catholic Church,
15.   the communion of saints,
16.   the forgiveness of sins,
17.   the resurrection of the body,
18.   and the life everlasting. Amen.

The ICET version of the Apostles' Creed (International Consultation on English Texts). *Prayers We Have in Common*, 2nd rev. ed. (Philadelphia: Fortress Press, 1975). The ICEL version of the Apostles' Creed (International Commission on English in the Liturgy) is identical.

TRANSLATION OF THE APOSTLES' CREED

1   I believe in God the Father all-powerful (all-sovereign)
    creator of heaven and earth

2   And in Jesus Christ
    his only son (one and only son)
    our Lord

3   Who was conceived by the Holy Spirit
    born of the virgin Mary

4   Suffered under Pontius Pilate
    was crucified
    was dead
    and was buried

5   He descended into hell (to the dead)

6   On the third day he rose (again) from the dead

7   He ascended into heaven
    is seated at the right hand of God the Father all-powerful (all sovereign)

8   From where he will come to judge the living (quick) and the dead

9   I believe in the Holy Spirit (Ghost)

10   The holy catholic church

11   The communion of saints
     the forgiveness of sins

12   The resurrection of the body (the flesh)
     and life eternal (everlasting)

My translation of the Latin, done in a more literal fashion. See Michael Novak's *Confessions of a Catholic* (San Francisco: Harper & Row, 1983), pp. 20–24. Novak conveniently gathers for easy comparison the English translations by Liturgical Press, Benziger Bros., and Helicon Press. His discussion of the English in the Sunday missalettes raises the question of adequate translation.

TRANSLATION OF THE APOSTLES' CREED

1   I believe in God the Father all-sovereign
     creator of heaven and earth

2   And in Jesus Christ
     his one and only son
     our Lord

3   Who was conceived by the Holy Spirit
     born to the virgin Mary

4   Suffered under Pontius Pilate
     was crucified
     was dead
     and was buried

5   He descended into the underworld

6   On the third day he rose from the dead

7   He ascended into heaven
     is seated at the right hand of God the Father all-sovereign

8   From where he will come to judge the living and the dead

9   I believe in the Holy Spirit

10 The holy catholic church

11 The communion of saints
     the forgiveness of sins

12 The resurrection of the body
     and life eternal

My translation of the Latin, done in a more free fashion.

NICENO-CONSTANTINOPOLITAN CREED

italics = not in Apostles' Creed

Credo in *unum* Deum
Patrem Omnipotentem (pantocrator)
Factorem coeli et terrae
visibilium omnium et invisibilium

Et in *unum* Dominum Jesum Christum
Filium *Dei unigenitum*
Qui ex Patre natum ante omnia saecula.
(Deum de Deo,) [not in the Greek] *lumen de lumine, Deum verum de Deo vero,*
Genitum, non factum, consubstantialem (homoousion) *Patri*
per quem omnia facta sunt.

Qui propter nos homines et propter nostram salutem
descendit de coelis
Et incarnatus est de Spiritu Sancto
ex Maria Virgine, *et homo factus est.*

Crucifixus etiam *pro nobis* sub Pontio Pilato
Passus et sepultus est

Et resurrexit tertia die, *secundum Scripturas*

Et ascendit in coelum, sedet ad dexteram Patris

Et iterum venturus est *cum gloria*
judicare vivos et mortuous
cujus regni non erit finis

Et in Spiritum Sanctum *Dominum et vivificantem*
qui ex Patre (Filioque) [not in the Greek] *procedit*
Qui cum Patre et Filio simul adoratur et conglorificatur
qui locutus est per prophetas

Et *unam,* sanctam, catholicam, et *apostolicam* Ecclesiam

Confiteor unum baptisma in remissionem peccatorum

Et expecto resurrectionem *mortuorum*

Et vitam *venturi saeculi.* Amen

The Latin of the Niceno-Constantinopolitan Creed was taken from Denzinger, no. 150, p. 67. Denzinger took it from the official standardized Latin text in the *Missale Romanum.*

ICET TRANSLATION

1. We believe in one God,
2.   the Father, the Almighty,
3.   maker of heaven and earth,
4.   of all that is, seen and unseen.
5. We believe in one Lord, Jesus Christ,
6.   the only Son of God,
7.   eternally begotten of the Father,
8.   God from God, Light from Light,
9.   true God from true God,
10.   begotten, not made,
11.   of one Being with the Father.
12.   Through him all things were made.
13.   For us men and for our salvation
14.   he came down from heaven:
15.   by the power of the Holy Spirit
16.   he became incarnate from the Virgin Mary and was made man.
17.   For our sake he was crucified under Pontius Pilate;
18.   he suffered death and was buried.
19.   On the third day he rose again
20.   in accordance with the Scriptures;
21.   he ascended into heaven
22.   and is seated at the right hand of the Father.
23. He will come again in glory to judge the living and the dead,
24.   and his kingdom will have no end.
25. We believe in the Holy Spirit, the Lord, the giver of life,
26.   who proceeds from the Father [and the Son].
27.   With the Father and the Son he is worshiped and glorified.
28.   He has spoken through the Prophets.
29.   We believe in one holy catholic and apostolic Church.
30.   We acknowledge one baptism for the forgiveness of sins.
31.   We look for the resurrection of the dead,
32.   and the life of the world to come. Amen.

ICET version of the Niceno-Constantinopolitan Creed. *Prayers We Have in Common* (Philadelphia: Fortress Press, 1975).

ICEL TRANSLATION

We believe in one God,
   the Father, the Almighty,
   maker of heaven and earth,
   of all that is seen and unseen.

We believe in one Lord, Jesus Christ,
   the only Son of God,
   eternally begotten of the Father,
   God from God, Light from Light,
   true God from true God,
   begotten, not made, one in Being with the Father.
   Through him all things were made.
   For us men and for our salvation
      he came down from heaven:
      by the power of the Holy Spirit
      he was born of the Virgin Mary, and became man.

For our sake he was crucified under Pontius Pilate;
   he suffered, died, and was buried.
   On the third day he rose again
      in fulfillment of the Scriptures;
   he ascended into heaven
      and is seated at the right hand of the Father.
He will come again in glory to judge the living and the dead,
   and his kingdom will have no end. _____ , *where original ended* 325

We believe in the Holy Spirit, the Lord, the giver of life,
   who proceeds from the Father and the Son.
   With the Father and the Son he is worshiped and glorified.
   He has spoken through the Prophets.
   We believe in one holy catholic and apostolic Church.
   We acknowledge one baptism for the forgiveness of sins.
   We look for the resurrection of the dead,
      and the life of the world to come. Amen.

added in 381

ICEL version of the Niceno-Constantinopolitan Creed. *Vatican II Sunday Missal*
(Boston: Daughters of St. Paul, 1974), pp. 596–97.

NICENO-CONSTANTINOPOLITAN CREED

italics = not in Apostles' Creed

I believe in *one* God
Father all-mighty (pantocrator)
Maker of heaven and earth,
    of all things visible and invisible.

And in *one* Lord Jesus Christ
His only Son
Who was born from the Father before all ages
(God from God) [not in the Greek], *light from light, true God from true God,*
Begotten, not made, one in substance (homoousion) *with the Father*
through whom everything is made.

Who on account of us human beings and because of our salvation
Came down from heaven
And was made flesh by the Holy Spirit from the Virgin Mary,
and was made man.

And He was crucified *for us* under Pontius Pilate
Suffered and was buried

The third day He rose up, *according to the Scriptures*

He ascended into heaven,
    and is seated at the right hand of the Father

From where he will come again *with glory*
to judge the living and the dead,
whose reign will never end.

And in the Holy Spirit *Lord and life-giver*
who from the Father (and the Son) [Filioque not in the Greek] *proceeds*
who with the Father and the Son is likewise adored and glorified
who has spoken through the prophets

And *one*, holy, catholic, and *apostolic* Church.

I confess one baptism for the forgiveness of sins.

And I await the resurrection of the *dead*

And the life *of the world to come.* Amen

    My translation.

ENGLAND: CIRCA A.D. 1125

Old English, Old French, and Latin

Ic gelefe on Gode Faedera aelwealdend
Ieo crei en Deu le Perre tut puant
Credo in Deum Patrem Omnipotentem

1

Sceppend heofones and eorthan
Le criatur de ciel e de terre
Creatorem coeli et terrae

— —

And on Helende Crist, Suna his anlich
E en Jesu Crist, sun Fil uniel
Et in Jesum Christum Filium ejus unicum

2

Drihten ure
Nostre Seinur
Dominum nostrum

— —

Syo the akynned is of tham Halig Gaste
Ki concevz est del Seint Esprit
Qui conceptus est de Spiritu Sancto

3

Boran of Marian tham maeden
Nez de Marie la [?]
Natus ex Maria Virgine

— —

Gethrowode under tham Pontiscam Pilate, and on rode ahangen
[?] ntien Pilate, crucifiez
Passus sub Pontio Pilato, crucifixus

4

Dead, and beberiged
Morz, e seveliz
Mortuus, et sepultus

— —

He adun astaeh to hellae
Descedied as enfers
Descendit ad inferna

5

197

Thriddan degge he aras fram deatha
Et tierz jurn relevad de morz
Tertia die resurrexit a mortuis

– –

He astah to heofone
Muntad as ciels
Ascendit ad coelos

6

Sit on switran healfe Godes Faederes ealmihtig
Siet a la destre de Deu Perre tres tut puant
Sedet ad dexteram Dei Patris omnipotentis

– –

Thanen he is to cumene, and to demenna quicke and deade
7　Diluc est avenir jugier les vis e les morz
Inde venturus judicare vivos et mortuos

– –

Ic gelefe on Halig Gast
8　Jeo crei el Seint Esprit
Credo in Spiritum Sanctum

– –

And on halig gesomnunge fulfremede
9　Seinte Eglise Catholica
Sanctam Ecclesiam Catholicam

– –

Halegan hiniennesse
La communion des seintes choses
Sanctorum communionem

10

Forgyfenysse synna
Remissium des pecchiez
Remissionem peccatorum

– –

Flesces up arisnesse
11　Resurrectiun de charn
Carnis resurrectionem

– –

Lif eche	Beo hit swa
12　Vie pardurable	Seit feit
Vitam aeternam	Amen

From Charles Heurtley, *Harmonia Symbolica: A Collection of Creeds* (Oxford: Oxford University Press, 1858), pp. 91–93. This creed is interesting for its early and uninhibited translations from the Latin.

ENGLAND A.D. 1543

I beleve in God the Father almighty,
Maker of heaven and earth;

And in Jesu Christe, his onely Sonne,
Our Lorde;

Whiche was conceived by the Holy Goste, Borne of the Virgine Mary;

Suffred under Ponce Pylate, was crucified,
Dead, buried,
And descended into Hell;

And the third day he rose agein from deth;

He ascended into heaven;
And sitteth on the right hand of God the Father almighty;

From thens he shall come to judge the quicke and the deade,

I beleve in the Holy Goste;

The holy Catholike Churche;

The communyon of sayntes;
The forgyveness of synnes;

The resurrection of the body;

And the lyfe everlastynge. Amen.

A post-Reformation English creed. From Heurtley, *Harmonia Symbolica*, p. 100.

OLD ENGLISH METRICAL VERSION OF
APOSTLES' CREED

I trow in God, fader of might,
    That alle has wroght,
Heven and erthe, day and night,
    And alle of noght.
And in Ihesu that God's Son is
    Al-onely,
Bothe God and mon, Lord endles,
    In him trow I;
Thurgh mekenes of tho holy gast,
    That was so milde,
He lyght in Mary mayden chast,
    Be-come a childe;
Under pounce pilat pyned he was,
    Us forto save,
Done on cros and deed he was,
    Layde in his grave;
The soul of him went into helle,
    Tho sothe to say;
Up he rose in flesshe and felle
    Tho tyryd day;
He stegh till heven with woundis wide,
    Thurgh his pouste;
Now sittes opon his fader right syde,
    In mageste;
Thethin shal he come us alle to deme
    In his manhede,
Qwyk and ded, alle that has ben
    In Adam sede,
Wel I trow in tho holi gost,
    And holi kirc that is so gode;

This metrical elaboration comes from Edgar Gibson's *The Three Creeds* (London: Longmans, Green, 1908), pp. 110–11. It is included here for the delight of the reader.

And so I trow that housel es
    Bothe flesshe and blode;
Of my synnes, forgyfnes,
    If I wil mende;
Up-risyng als-so of my flesshe,
    And lyf with-outen ende.